Valentine's Day

DOT MARKERS

ACTIVITY BOOK

35 VALENTINE'S DAY ILLUSTRATIONS TO COLOR WITH DOR MAKERS

THIS BOOK BELONGS TO

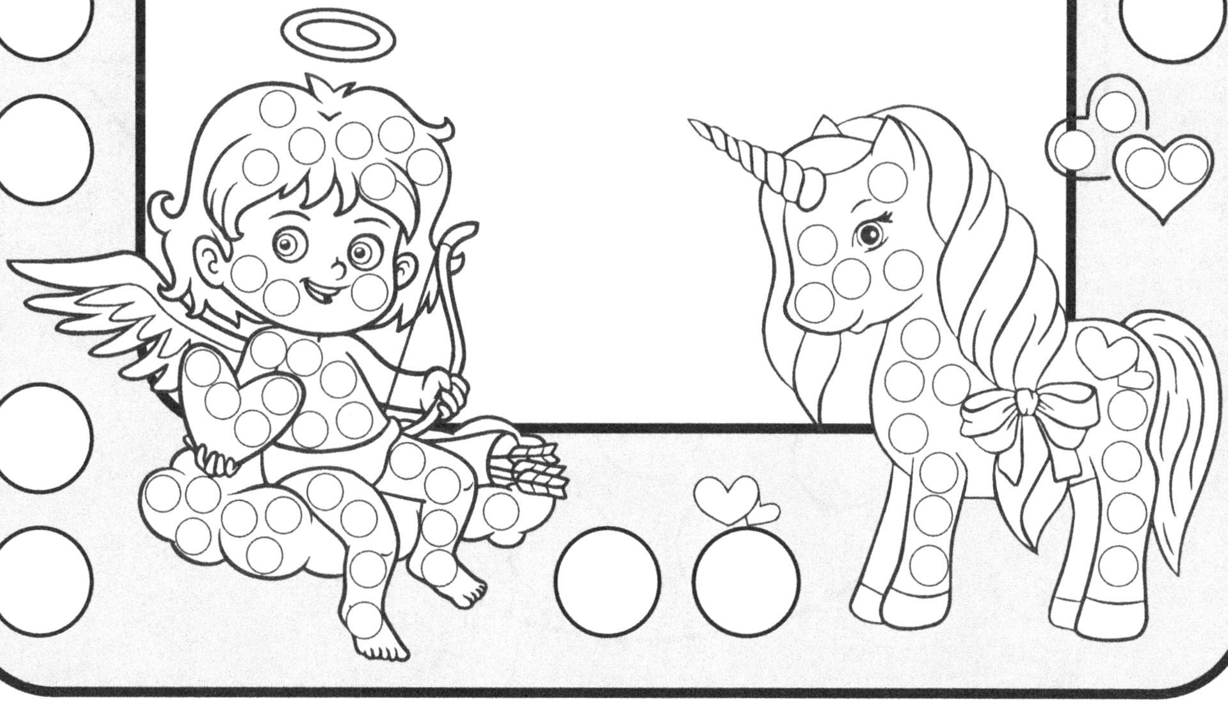

LET'S PRACTICE WITH DOT MARKERS!

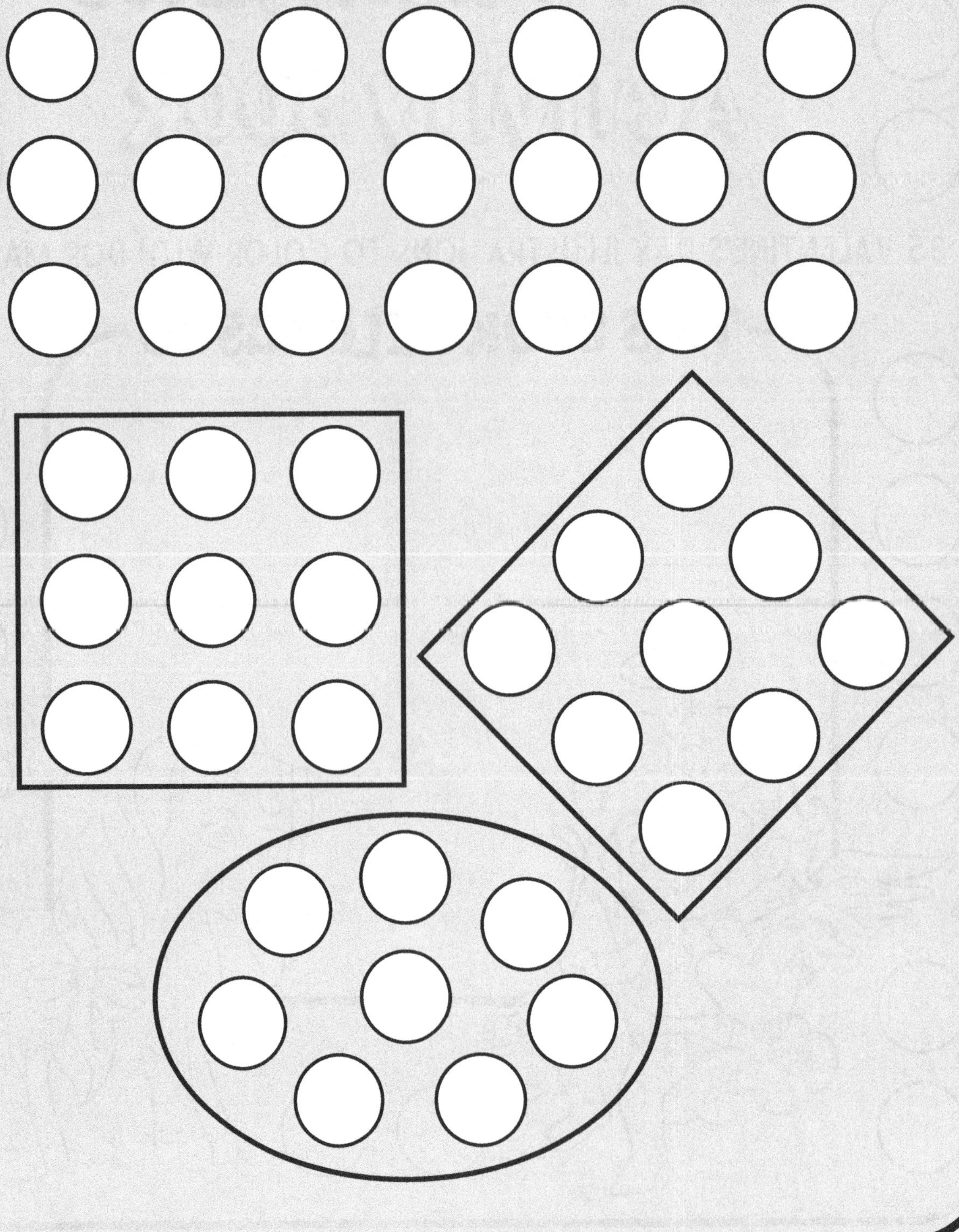

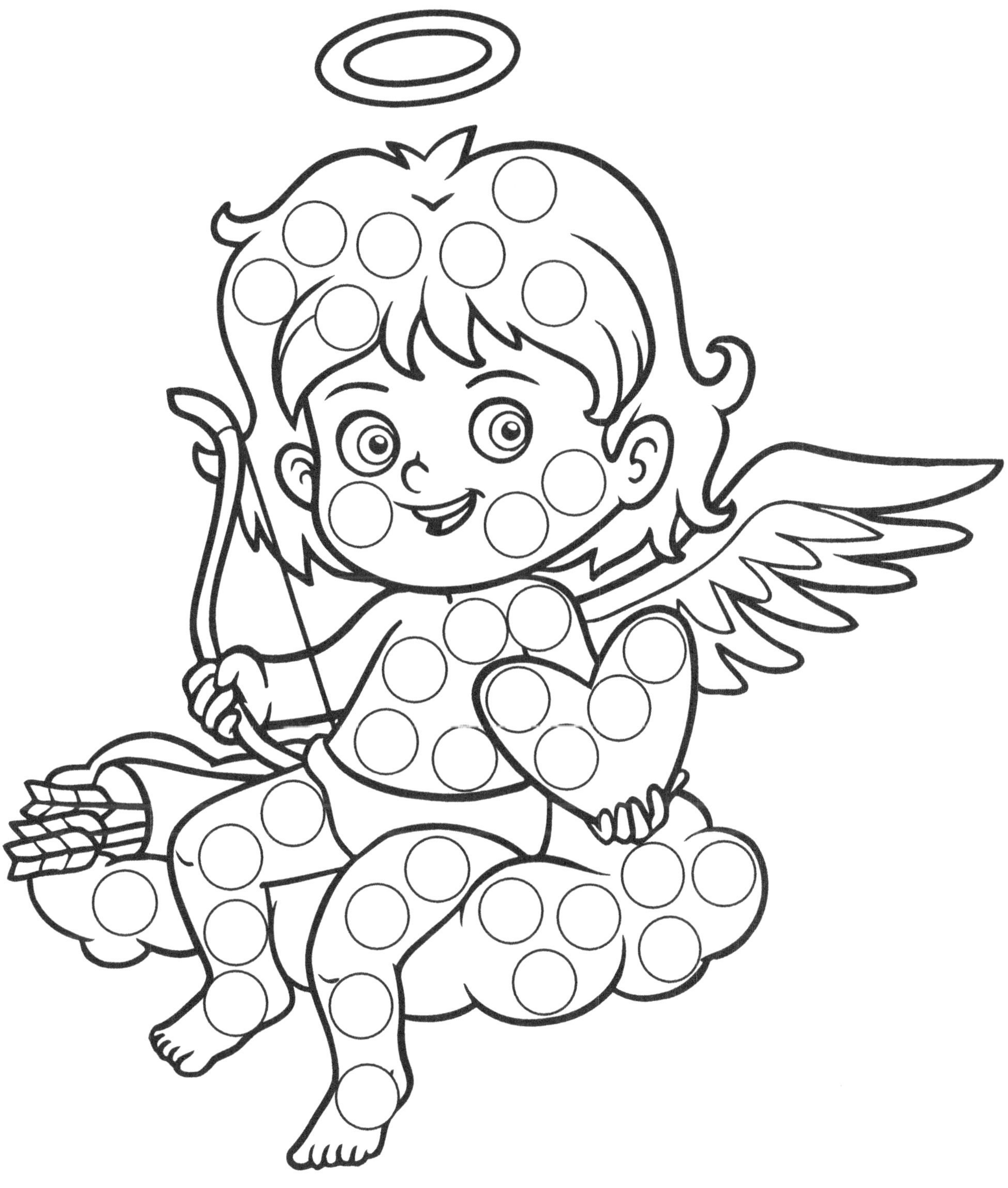

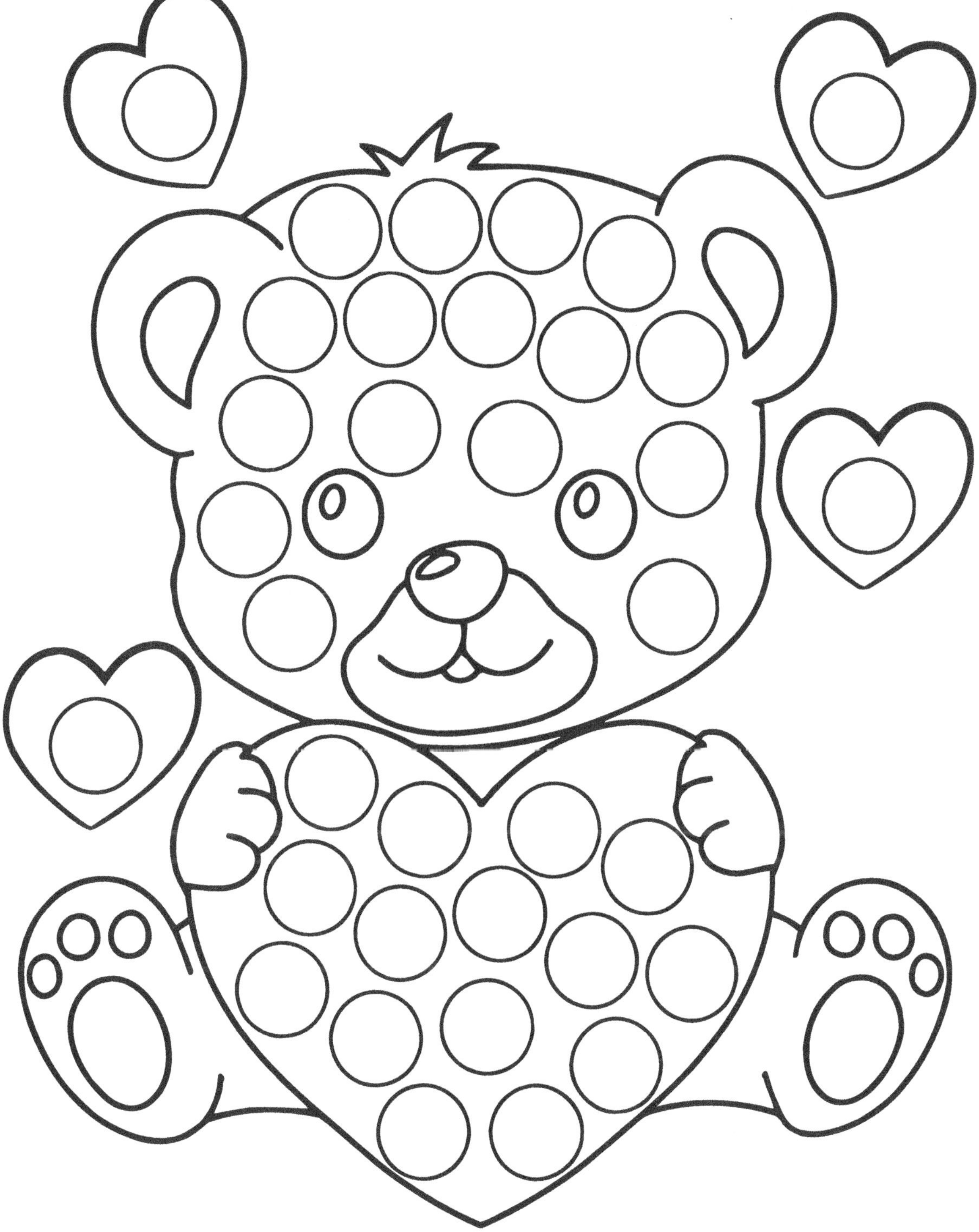

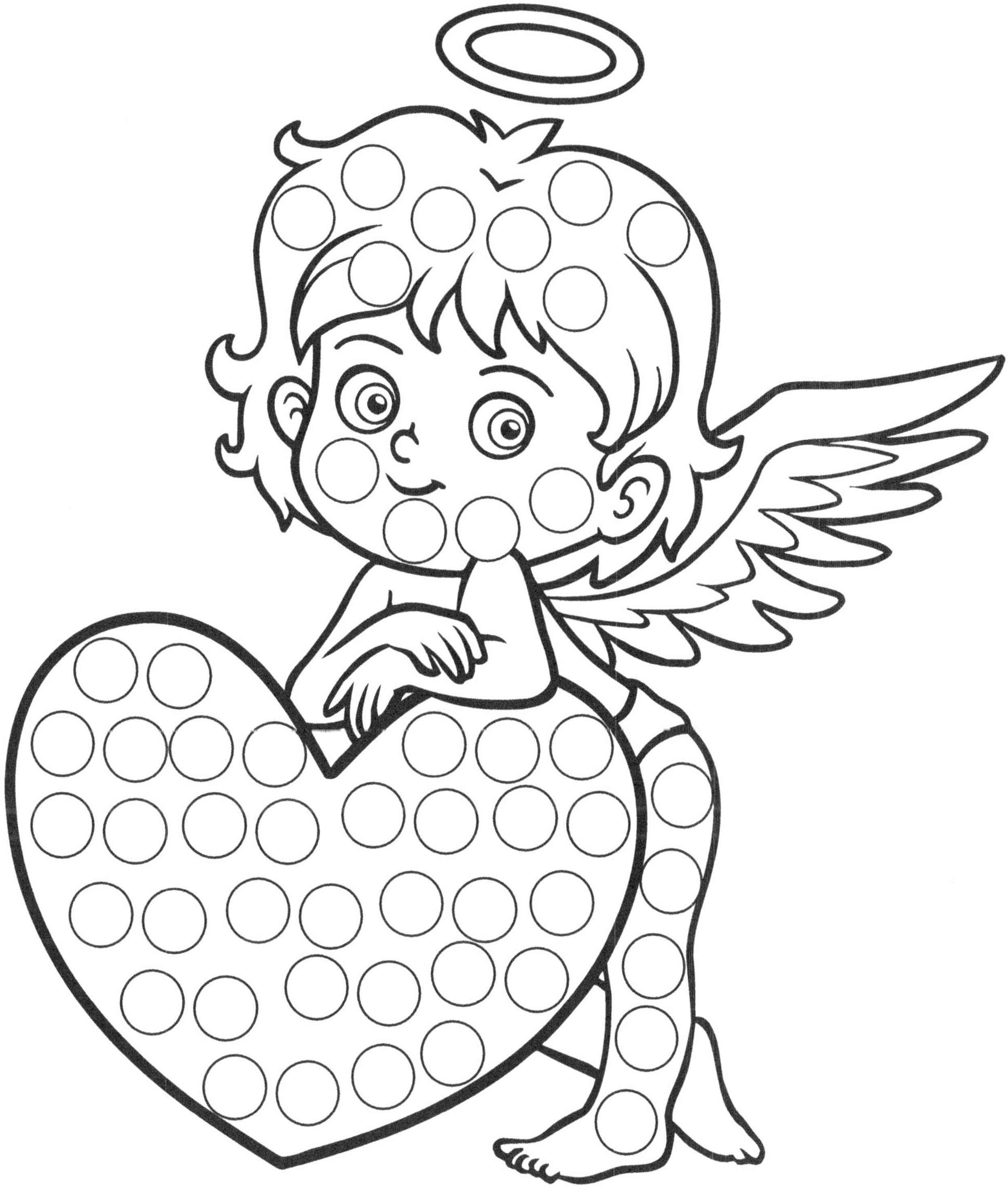

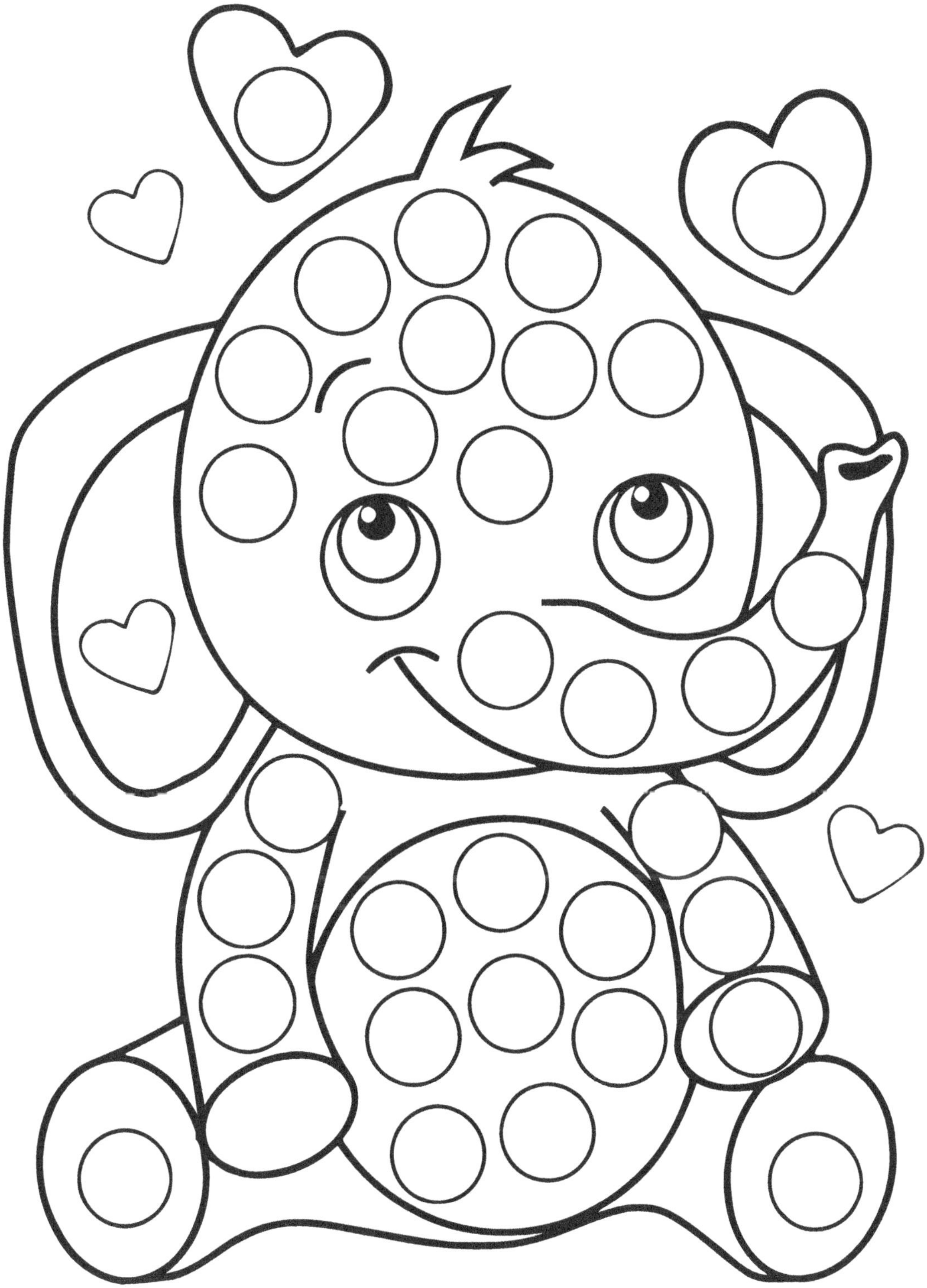

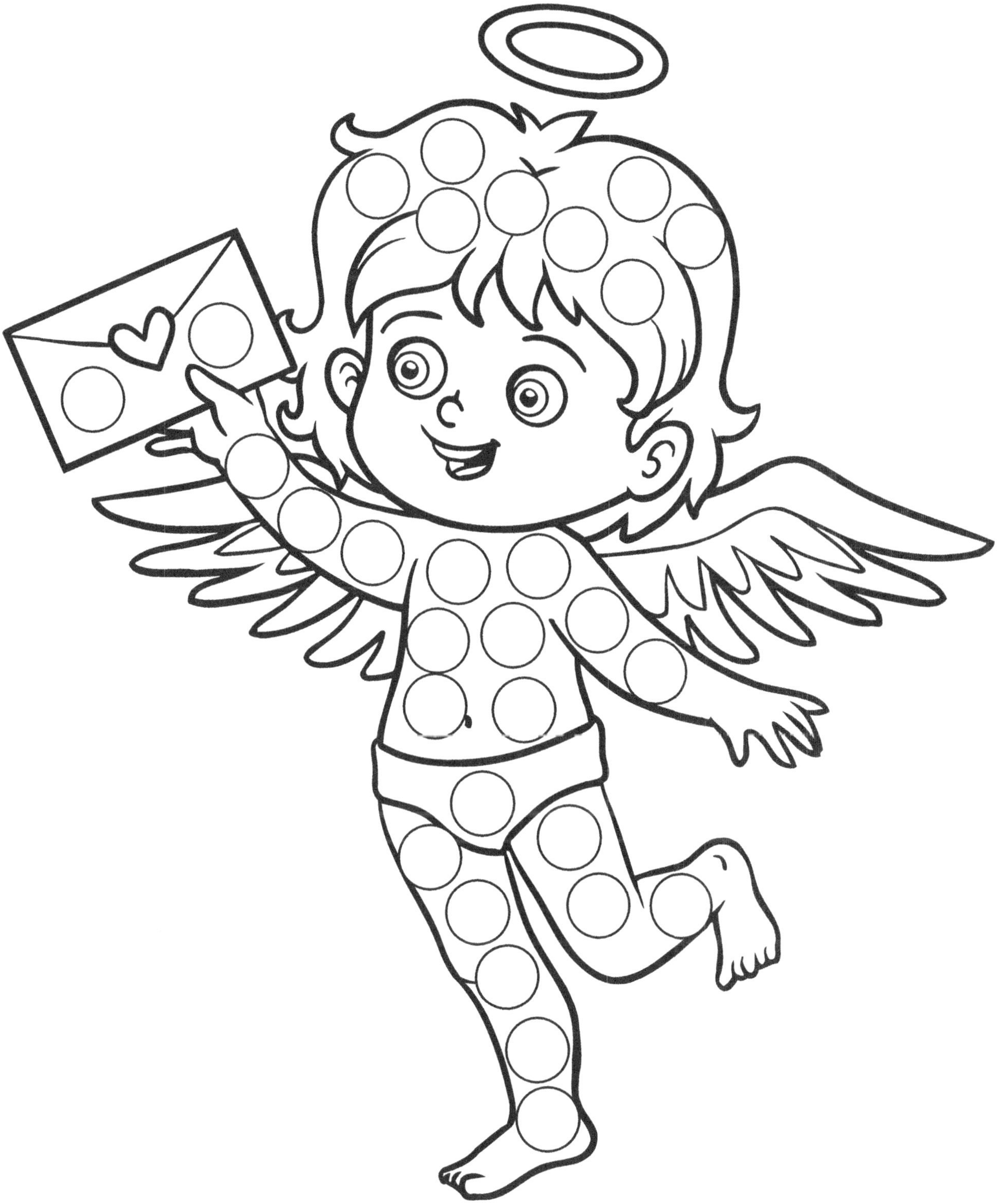

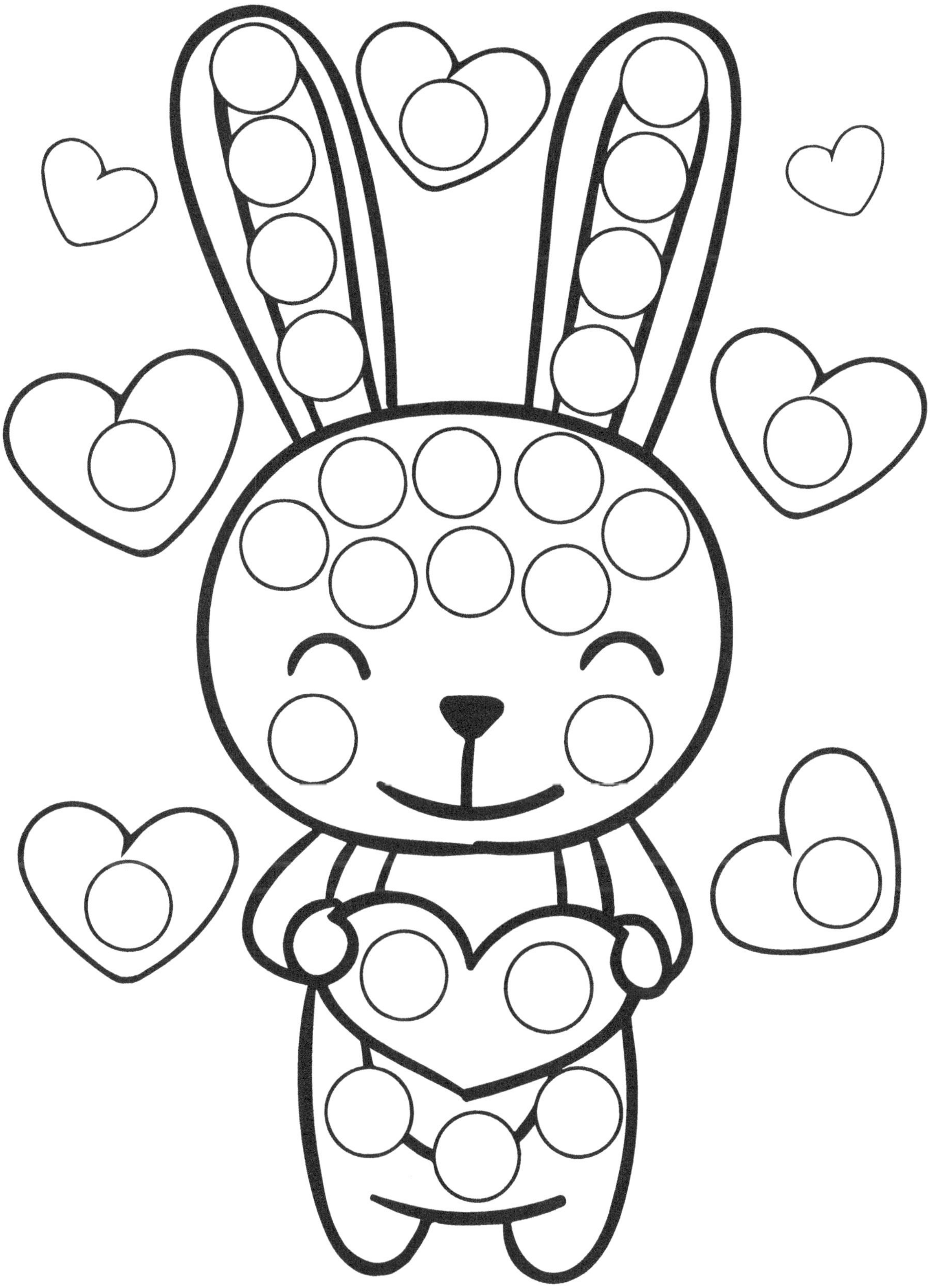

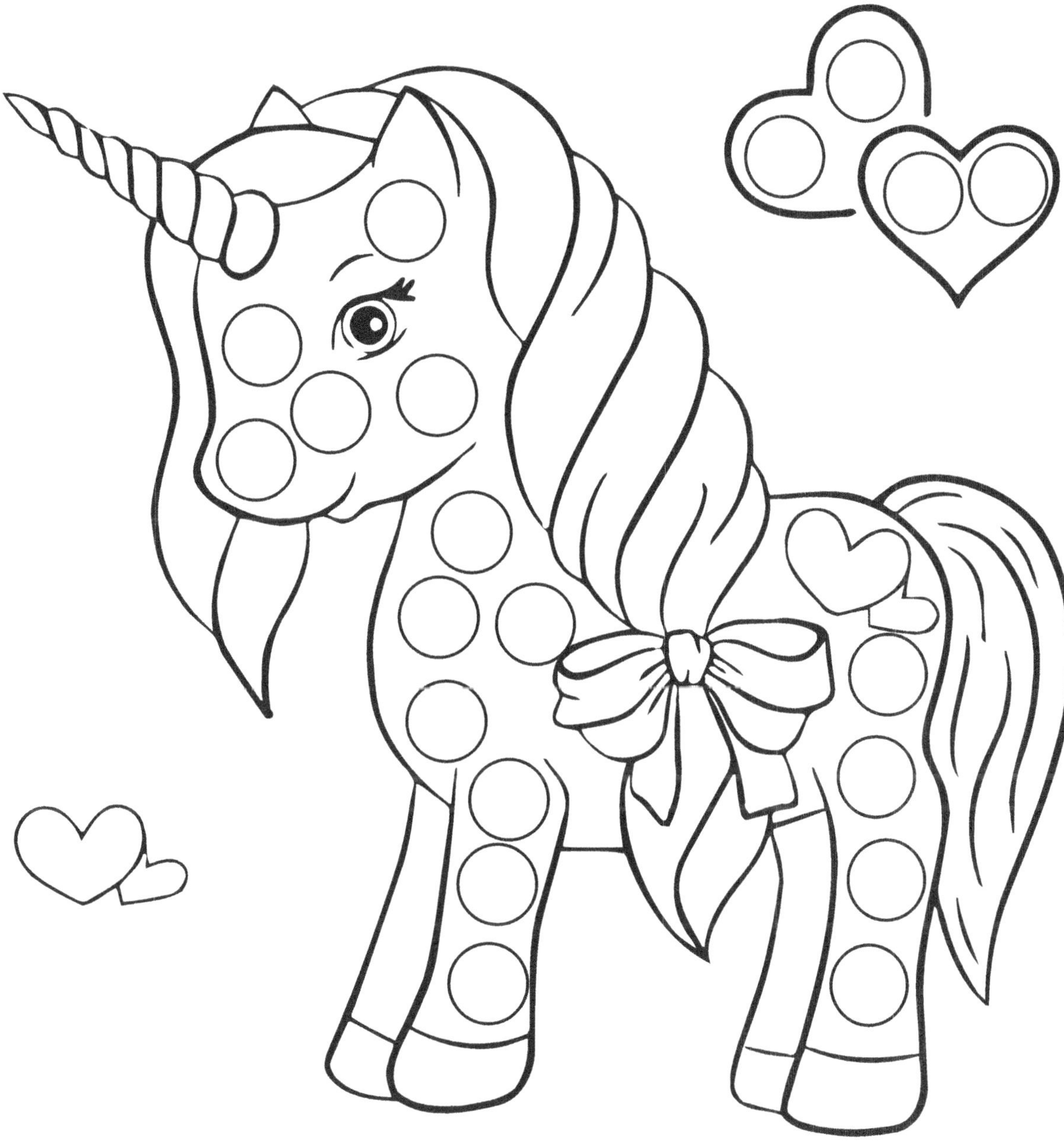

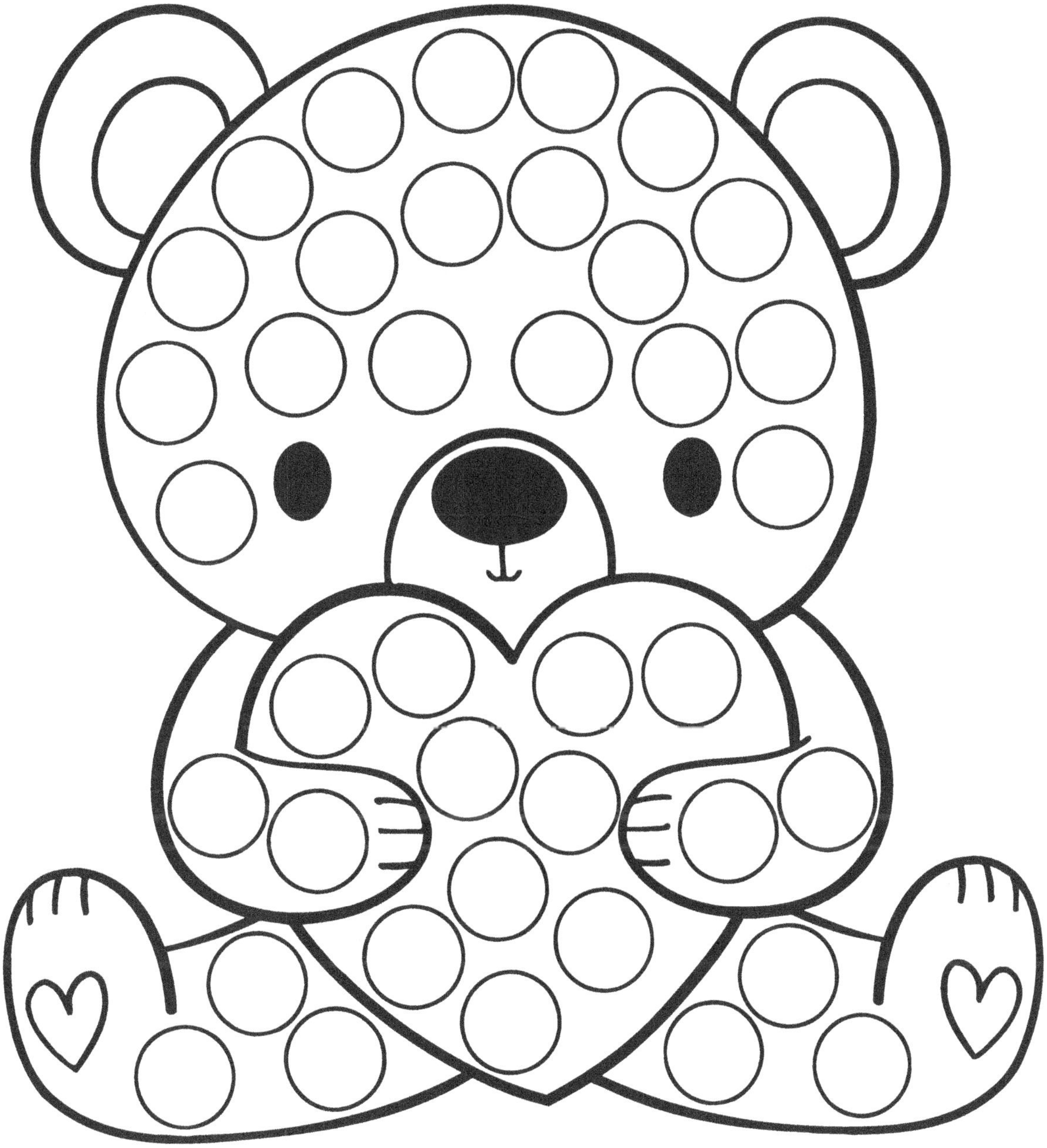

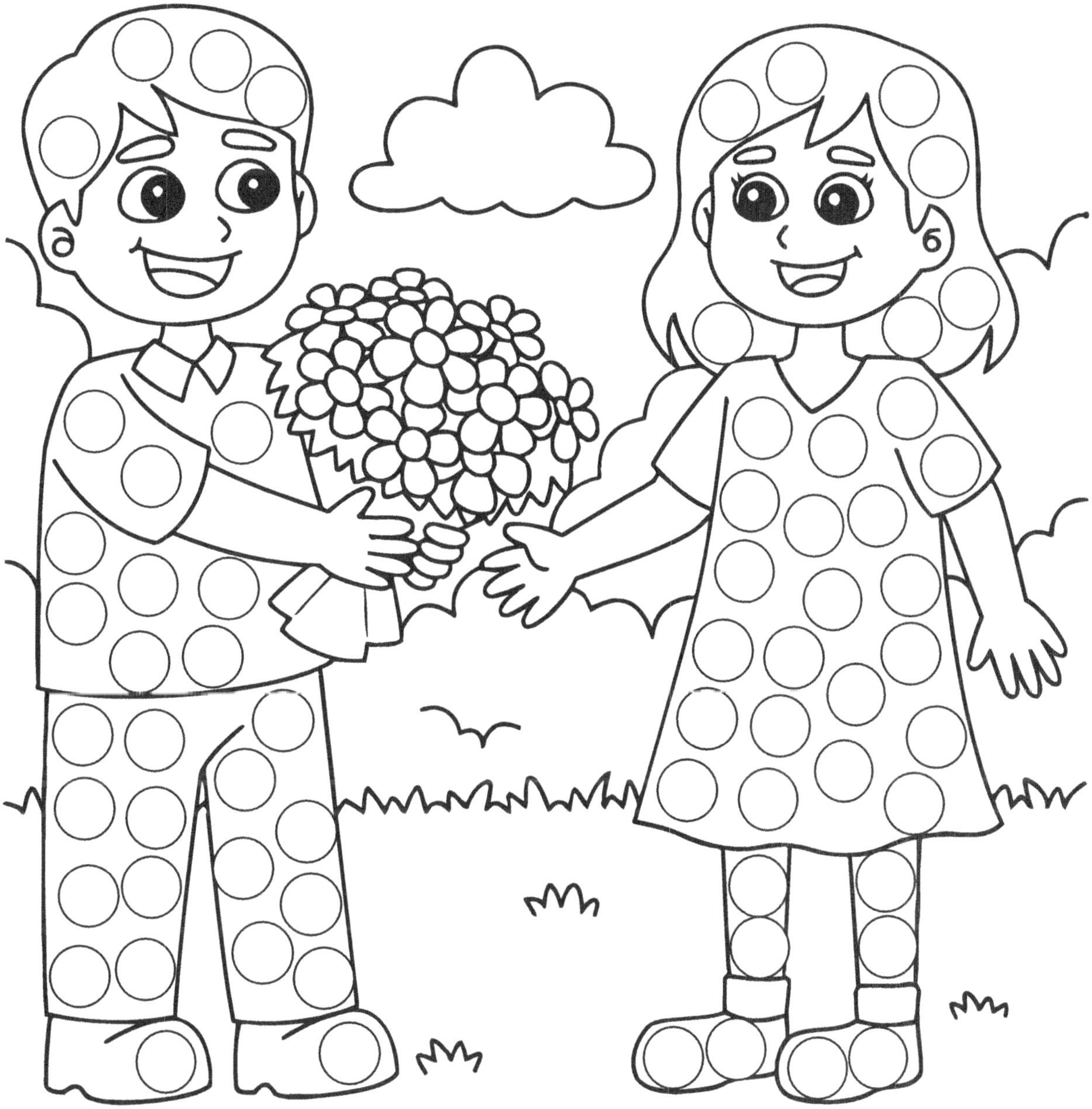

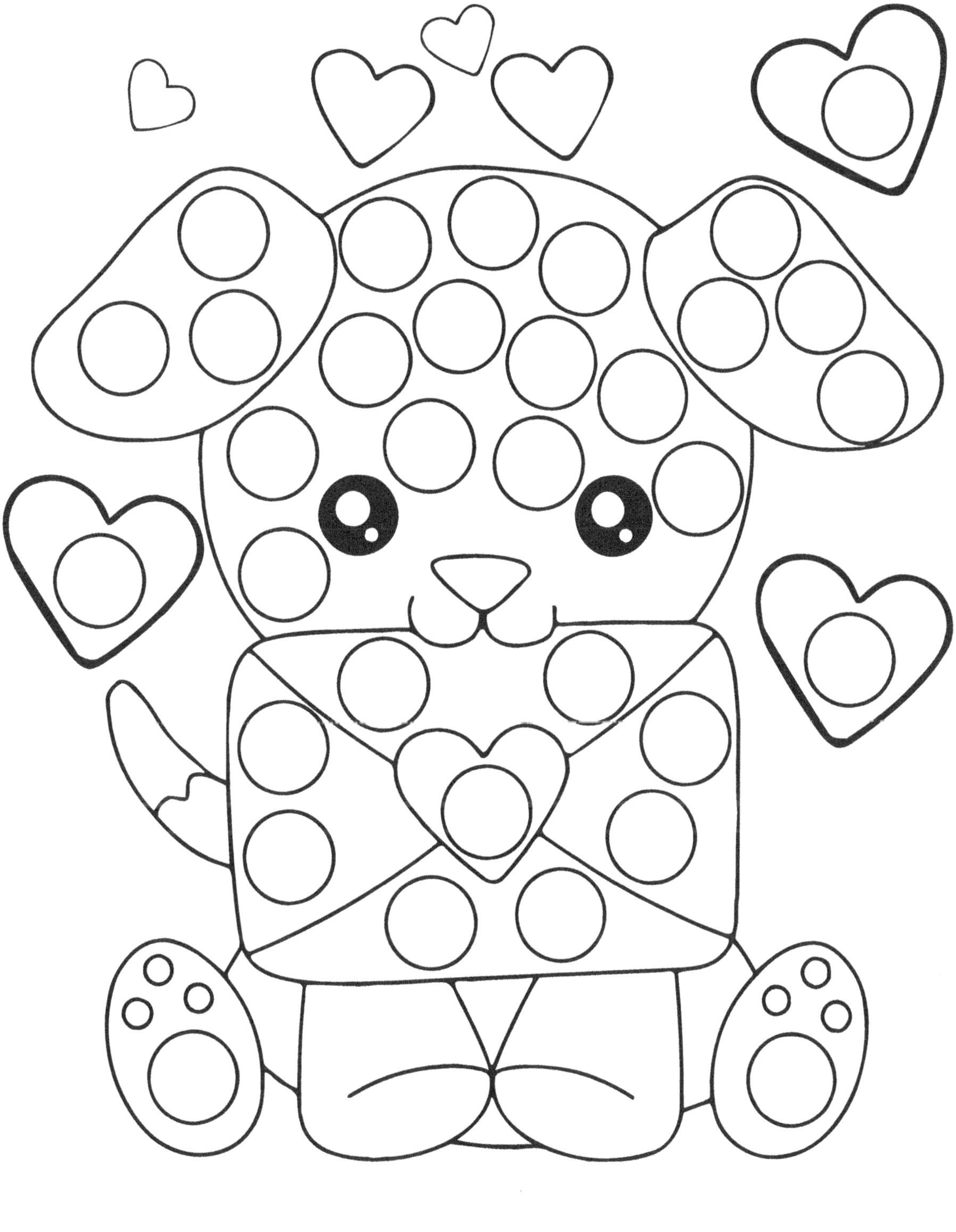

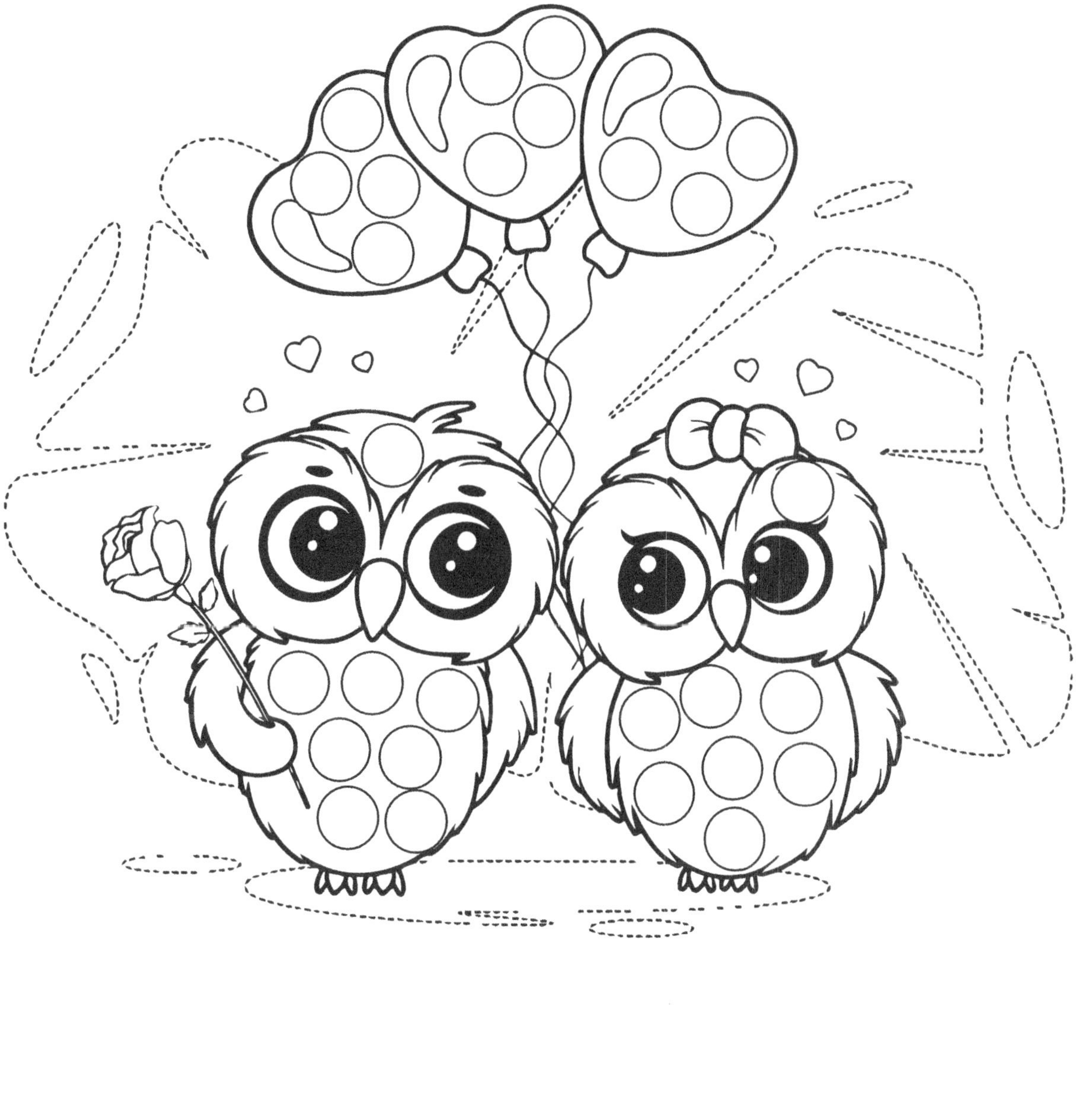

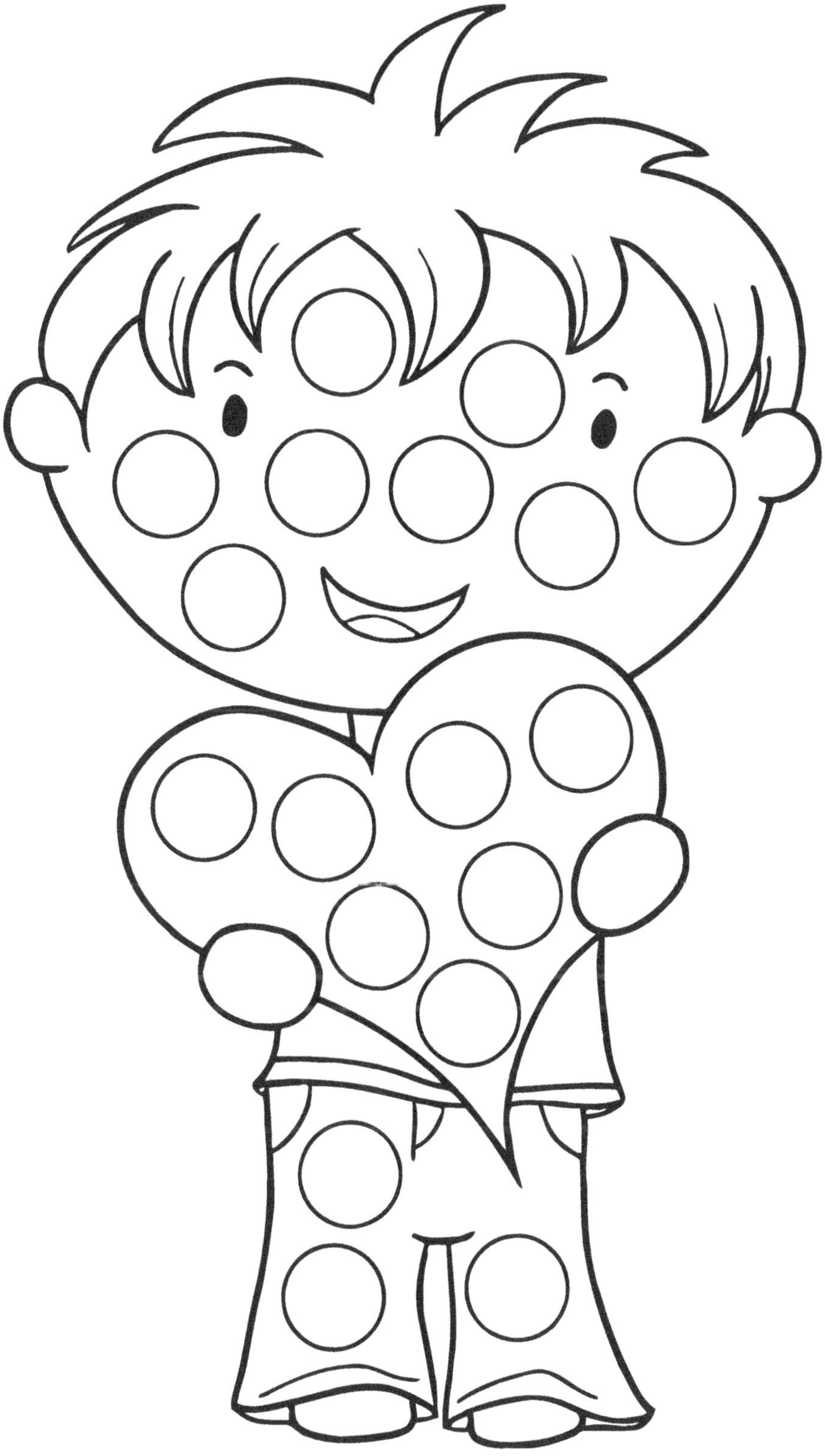

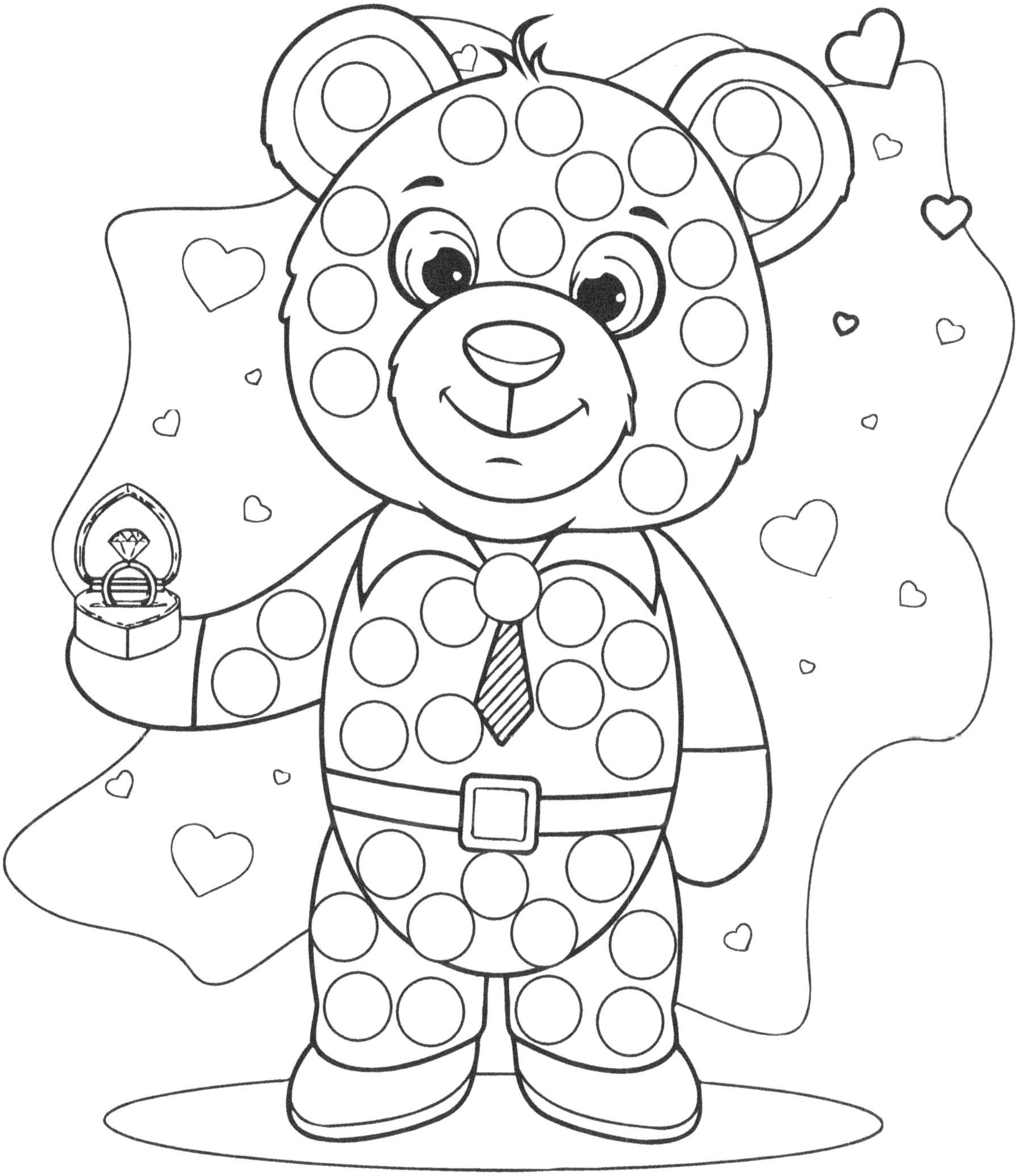

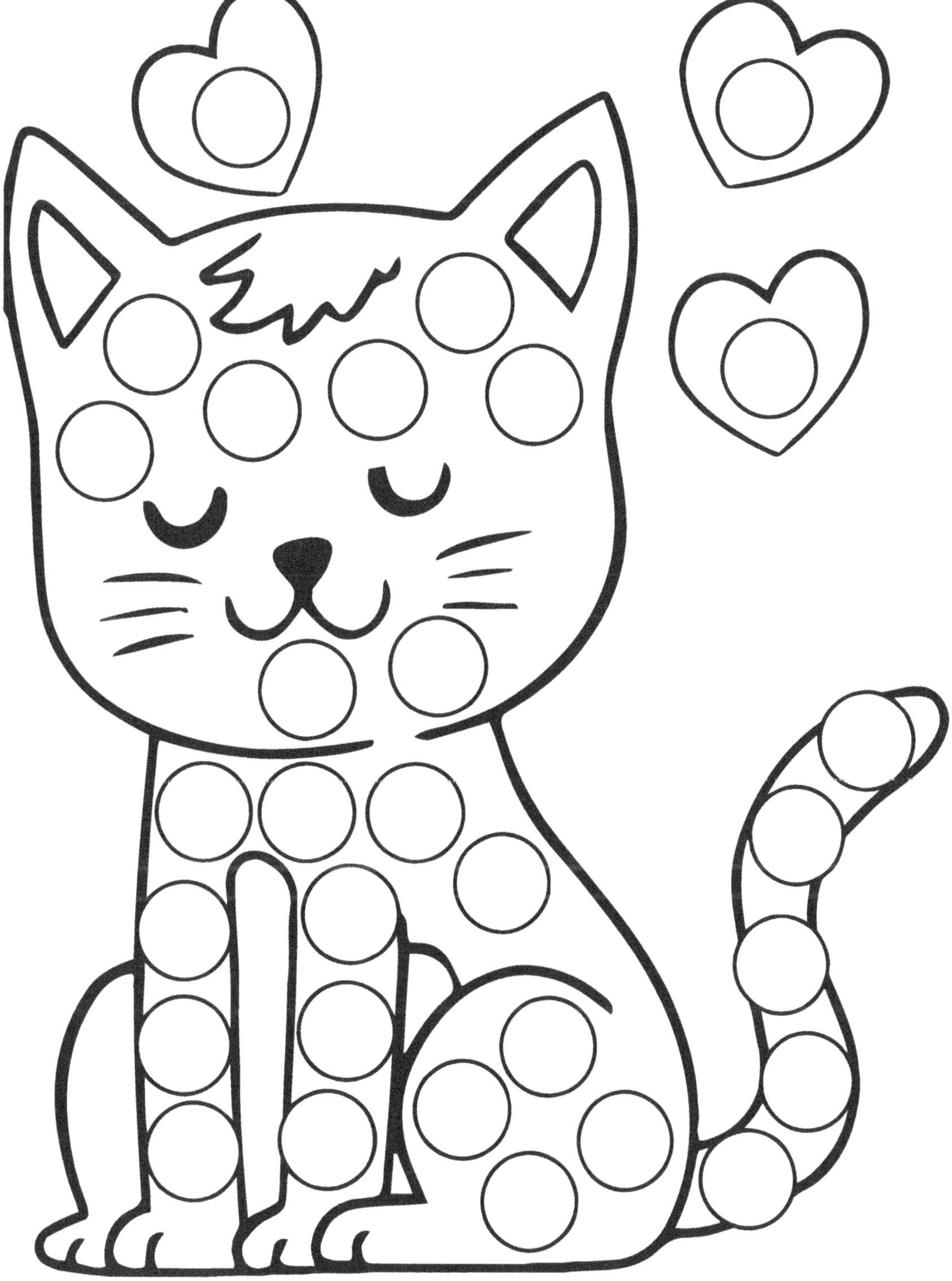

Happy Valentine's Day!

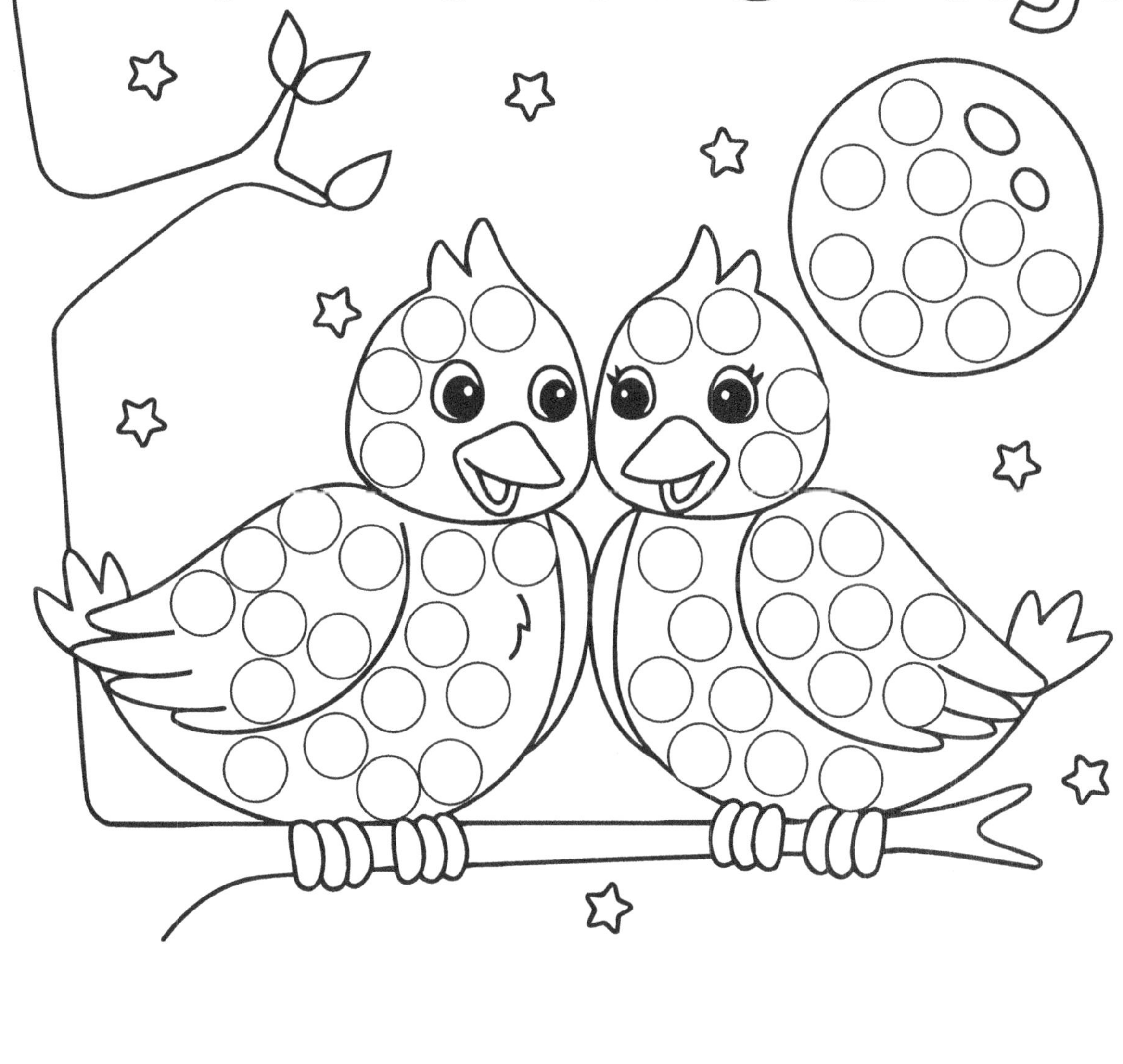

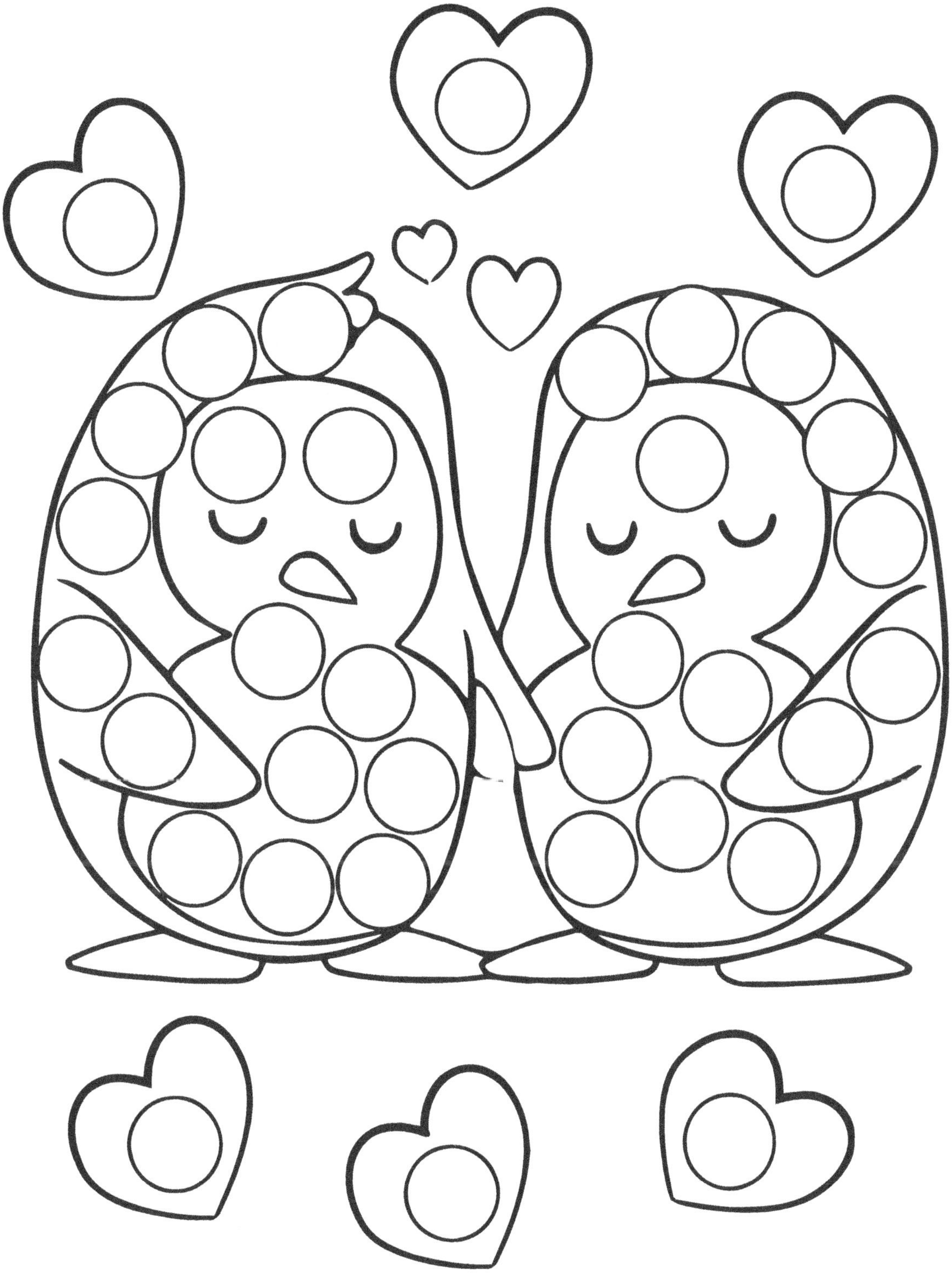

BEE MY VALENTINE

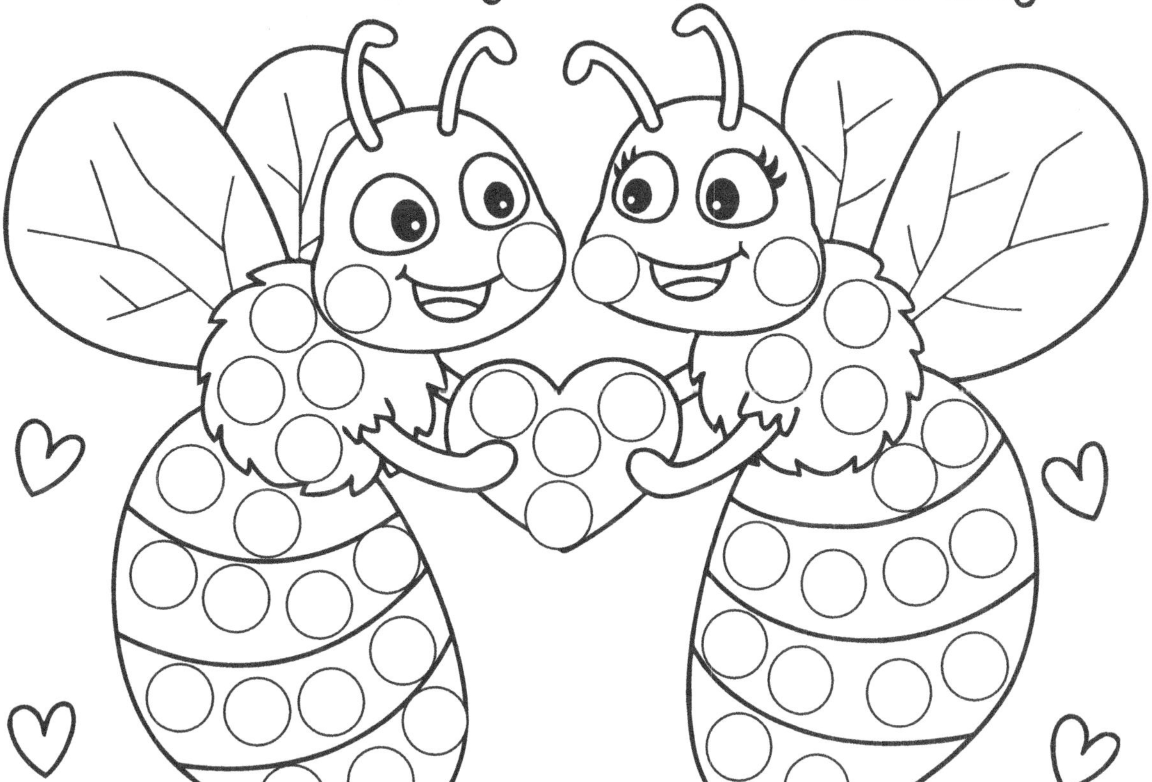

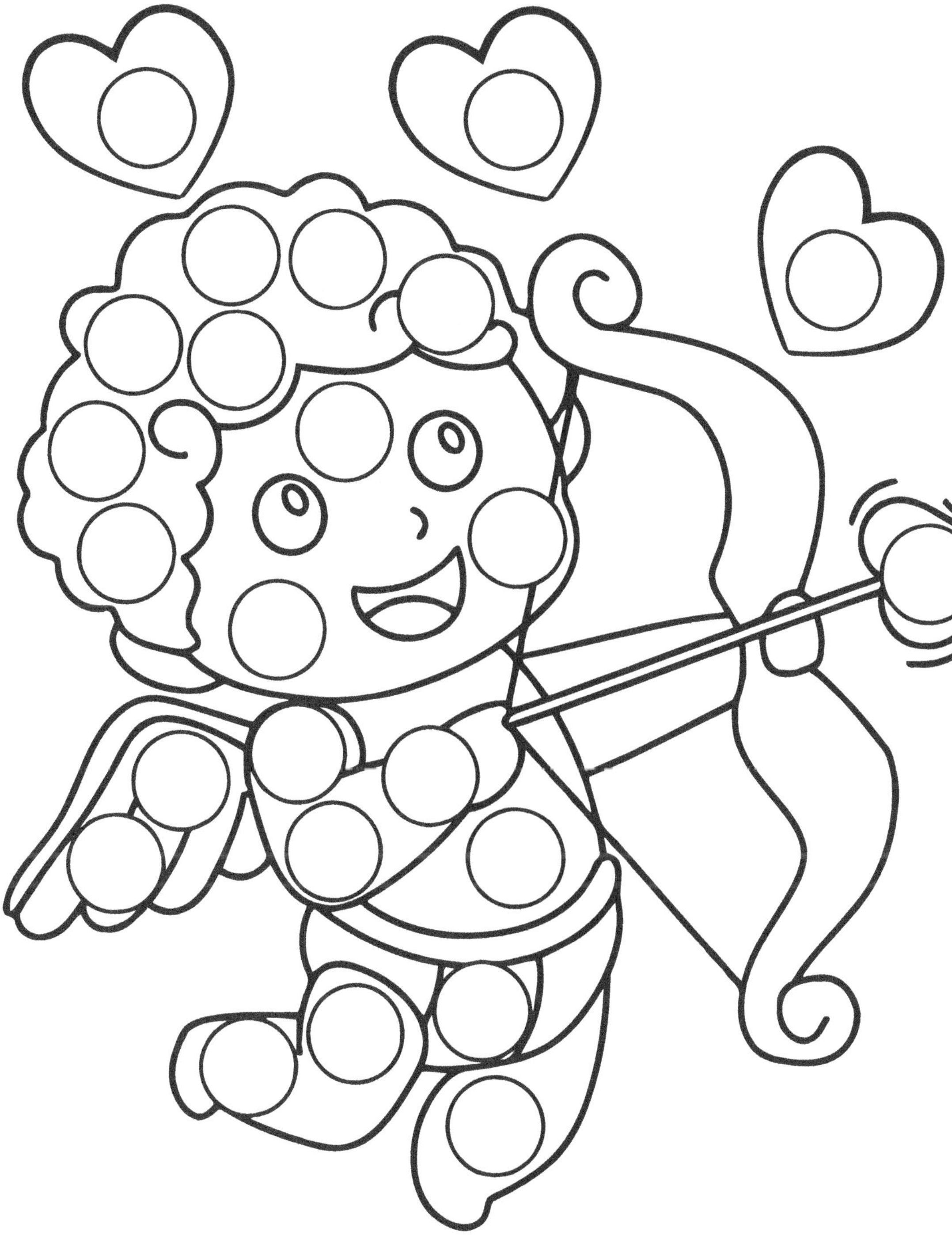

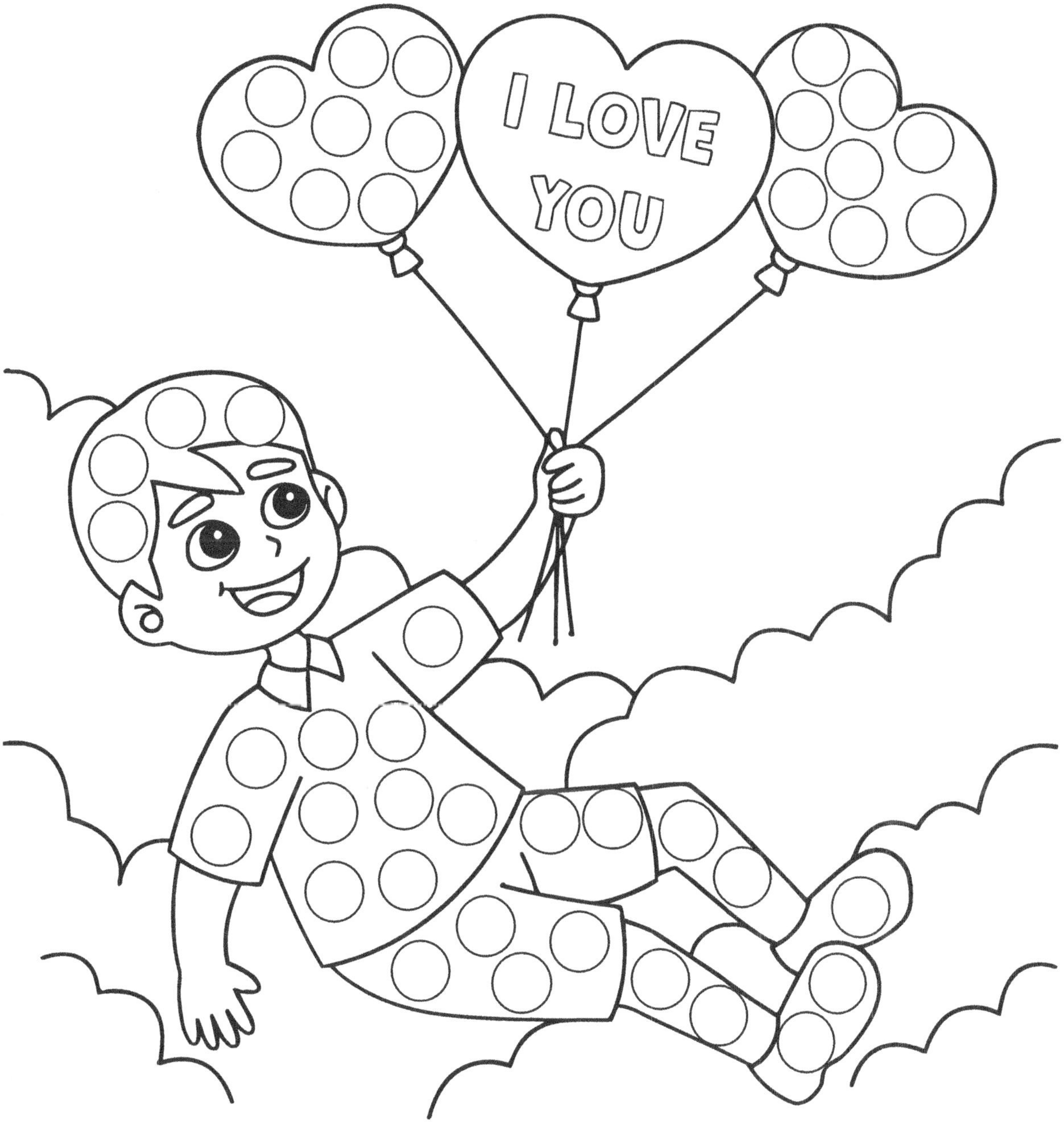
I LOVE YOU

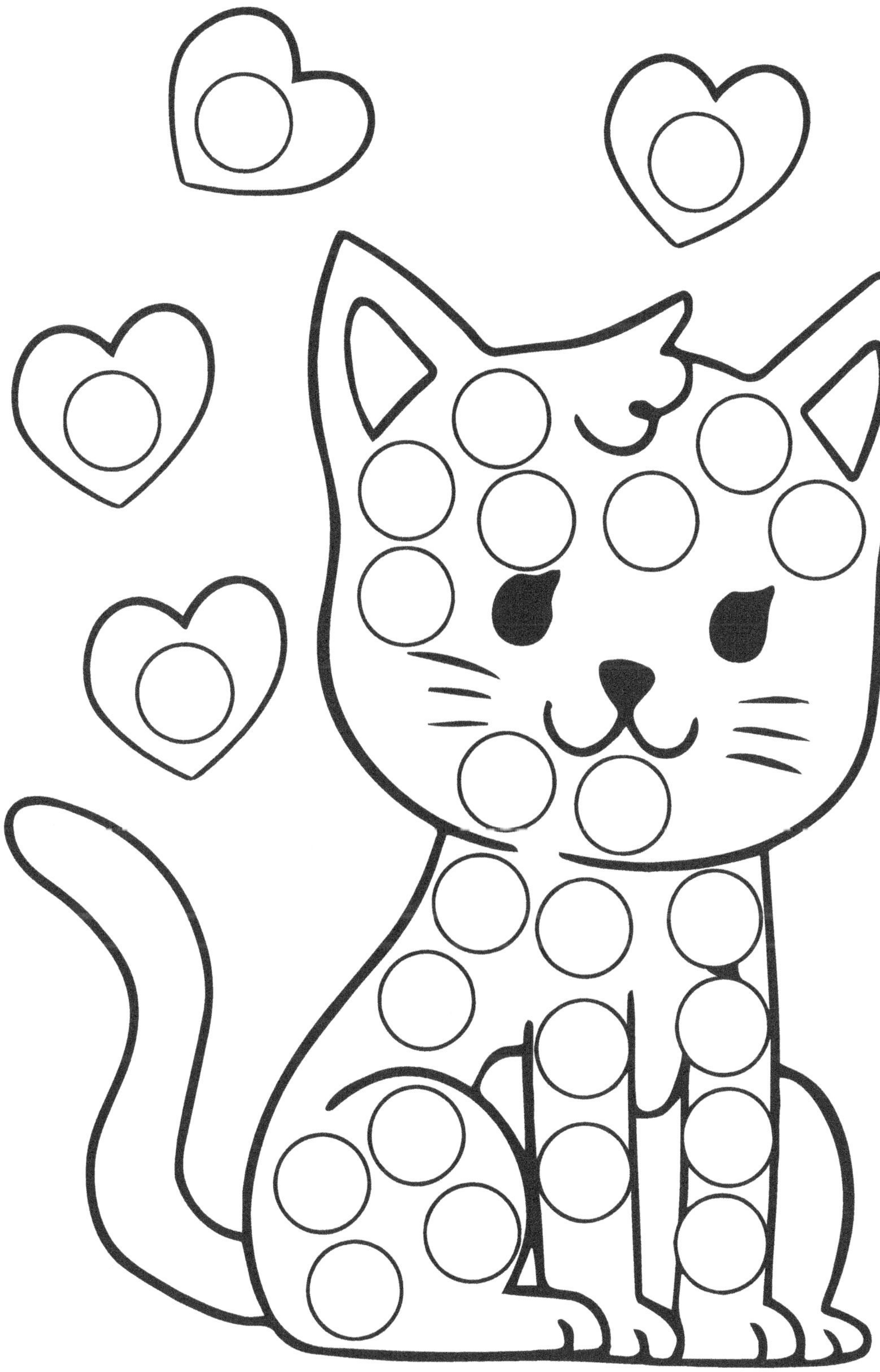

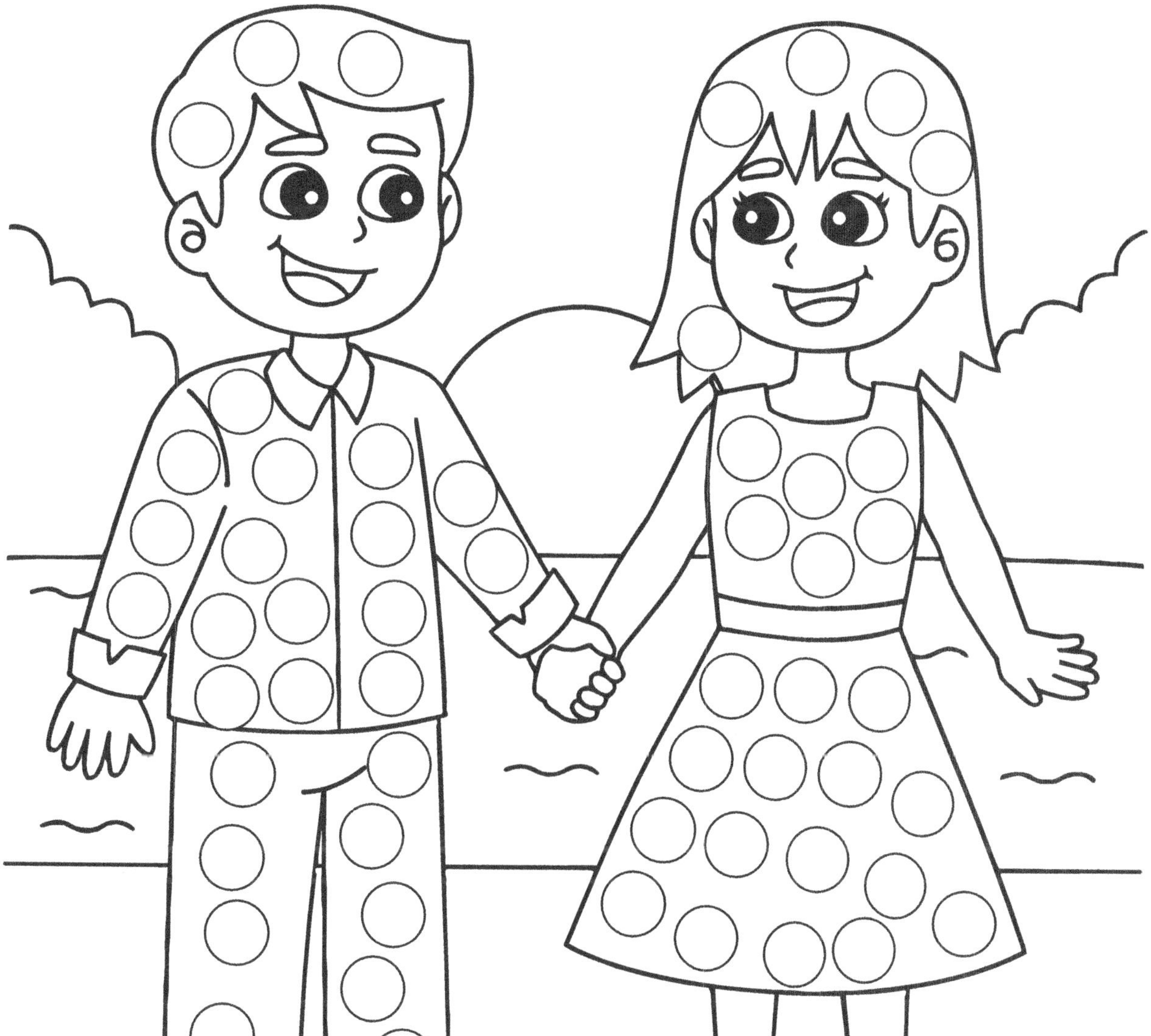

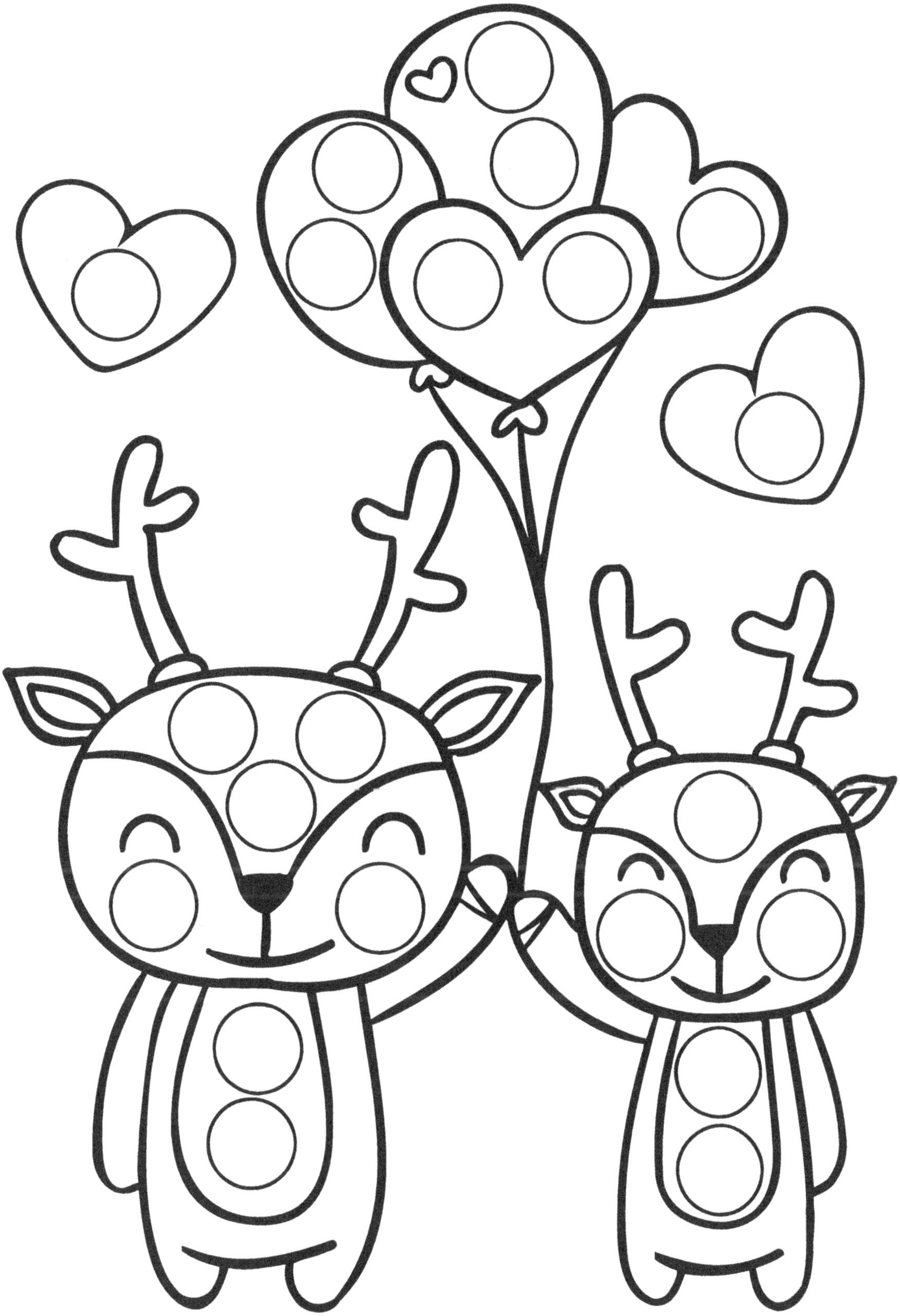

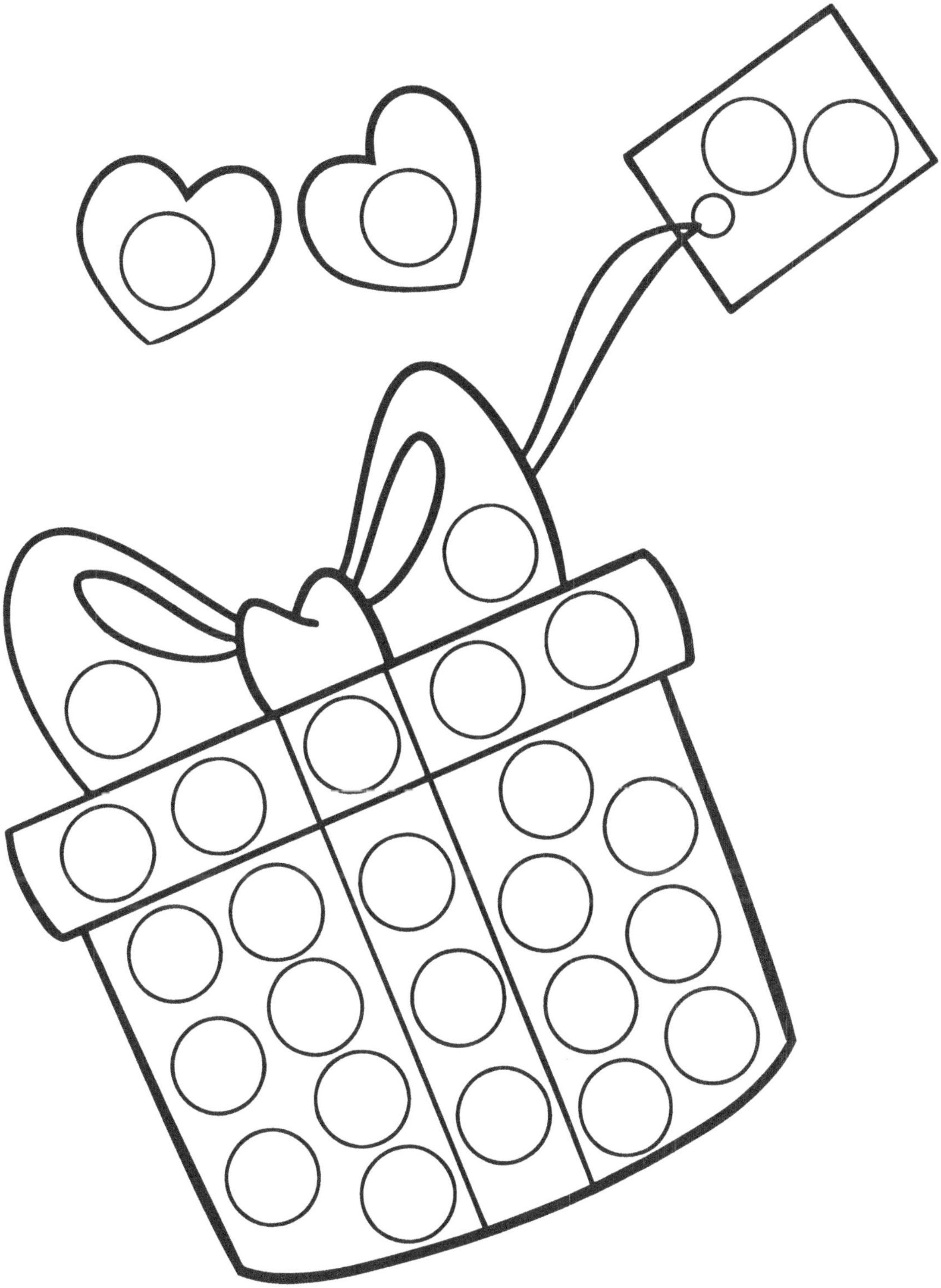

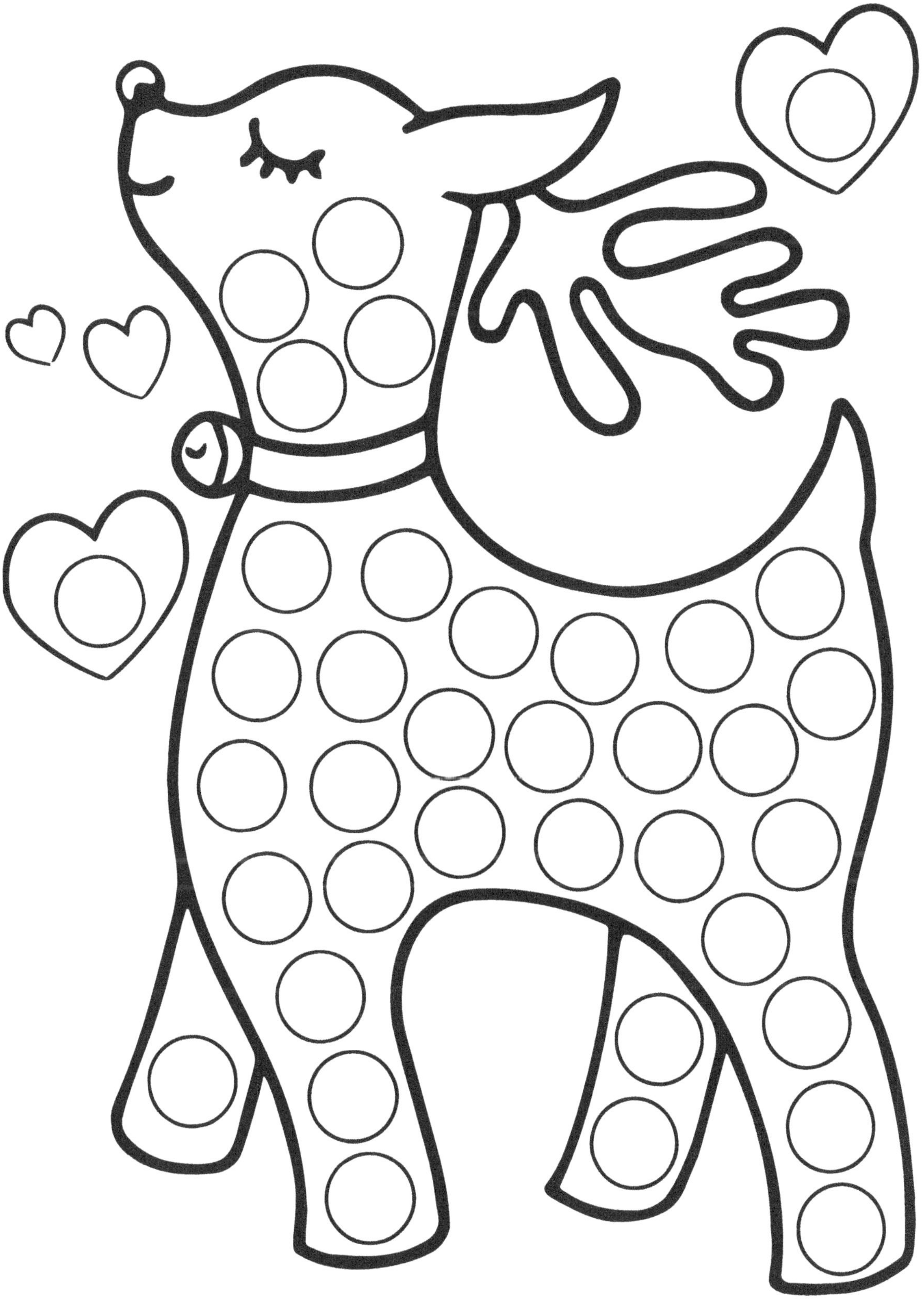

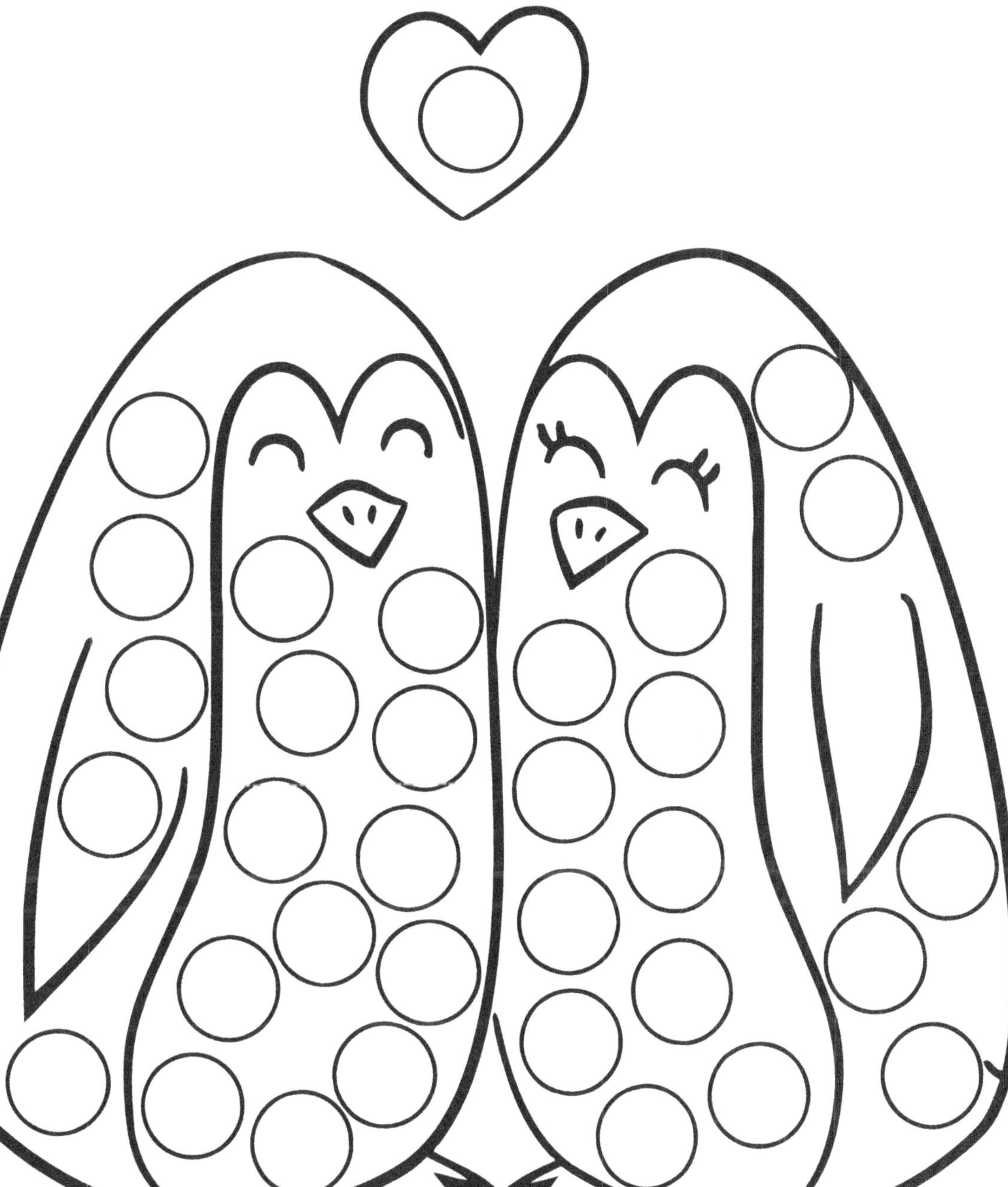

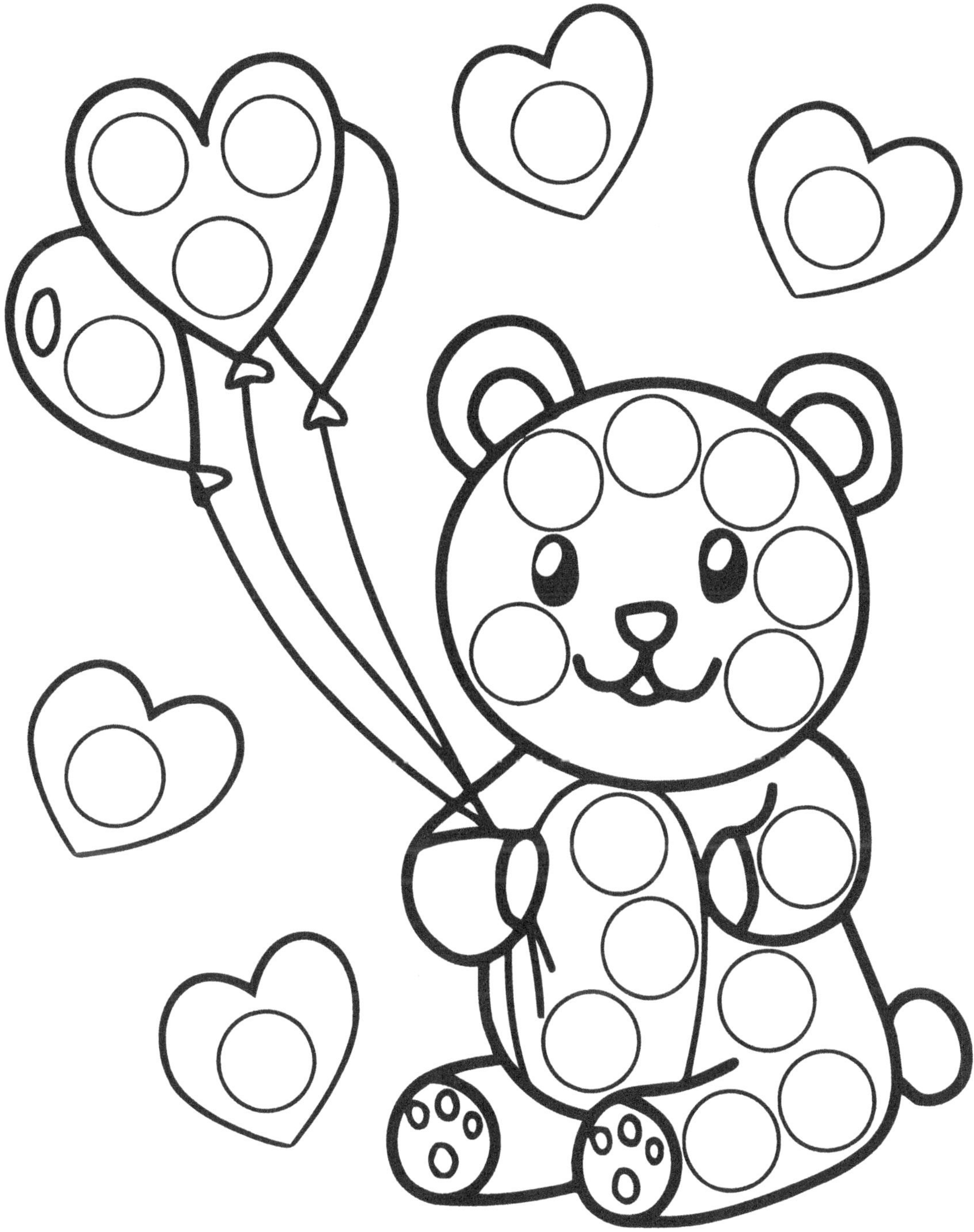

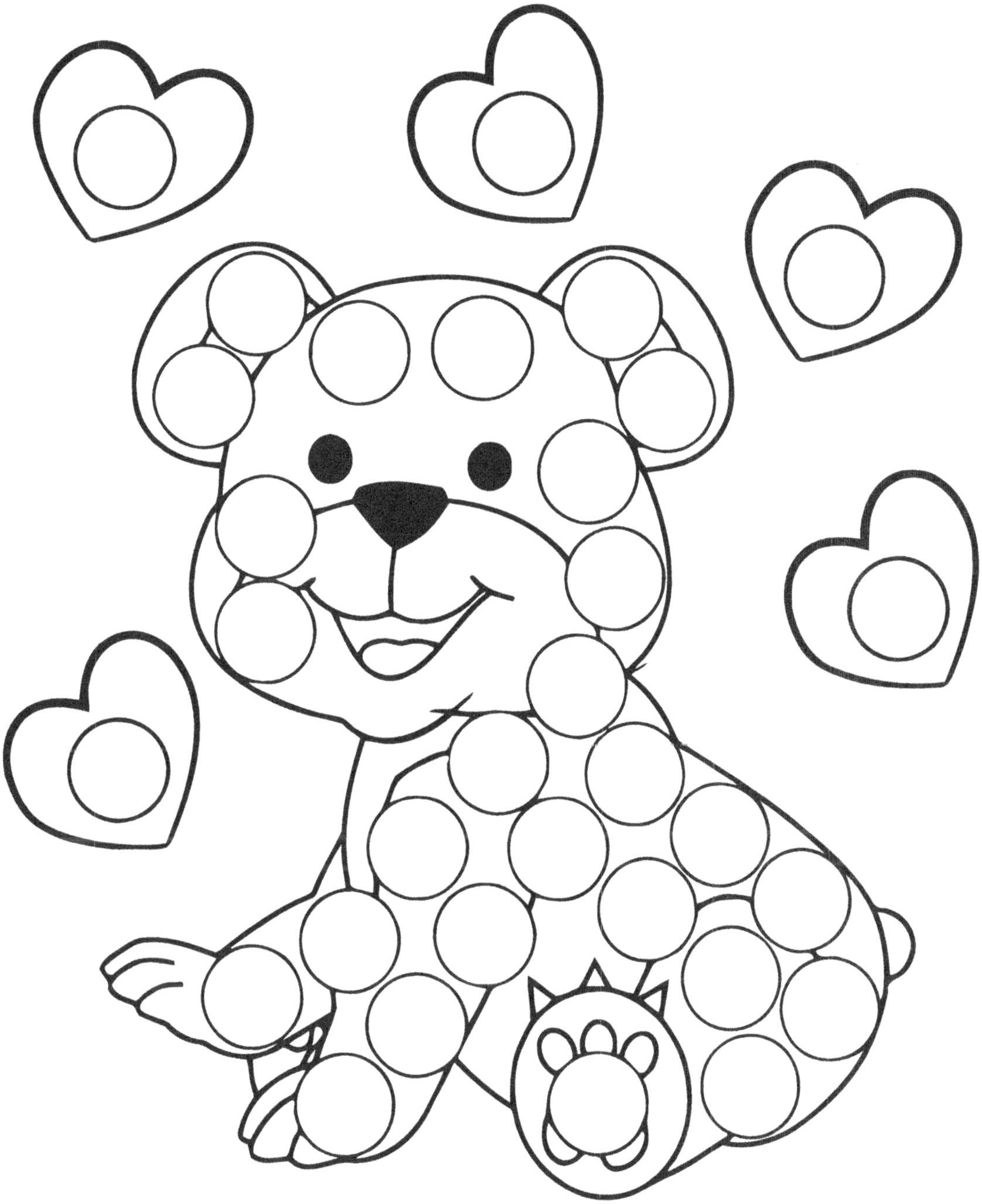

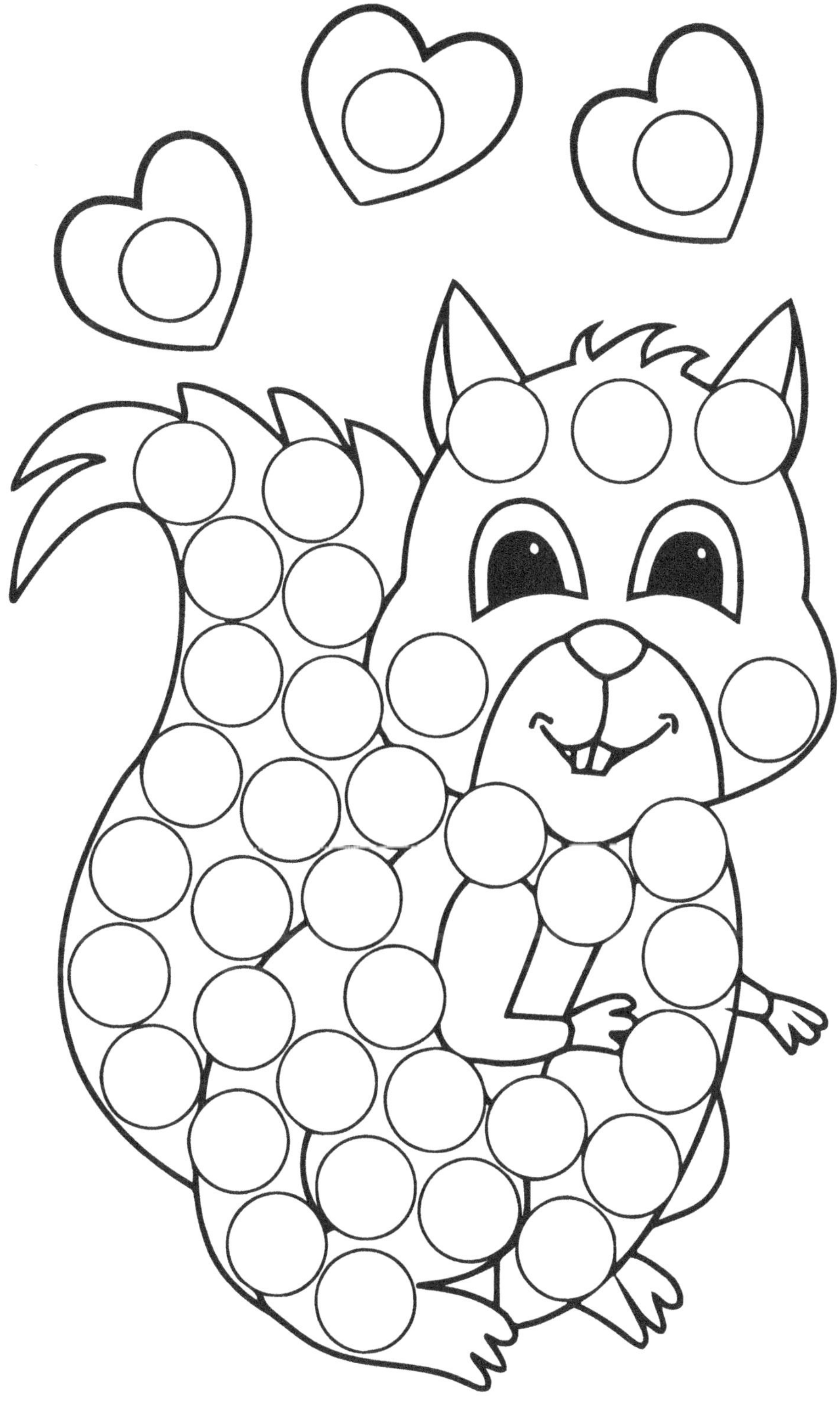

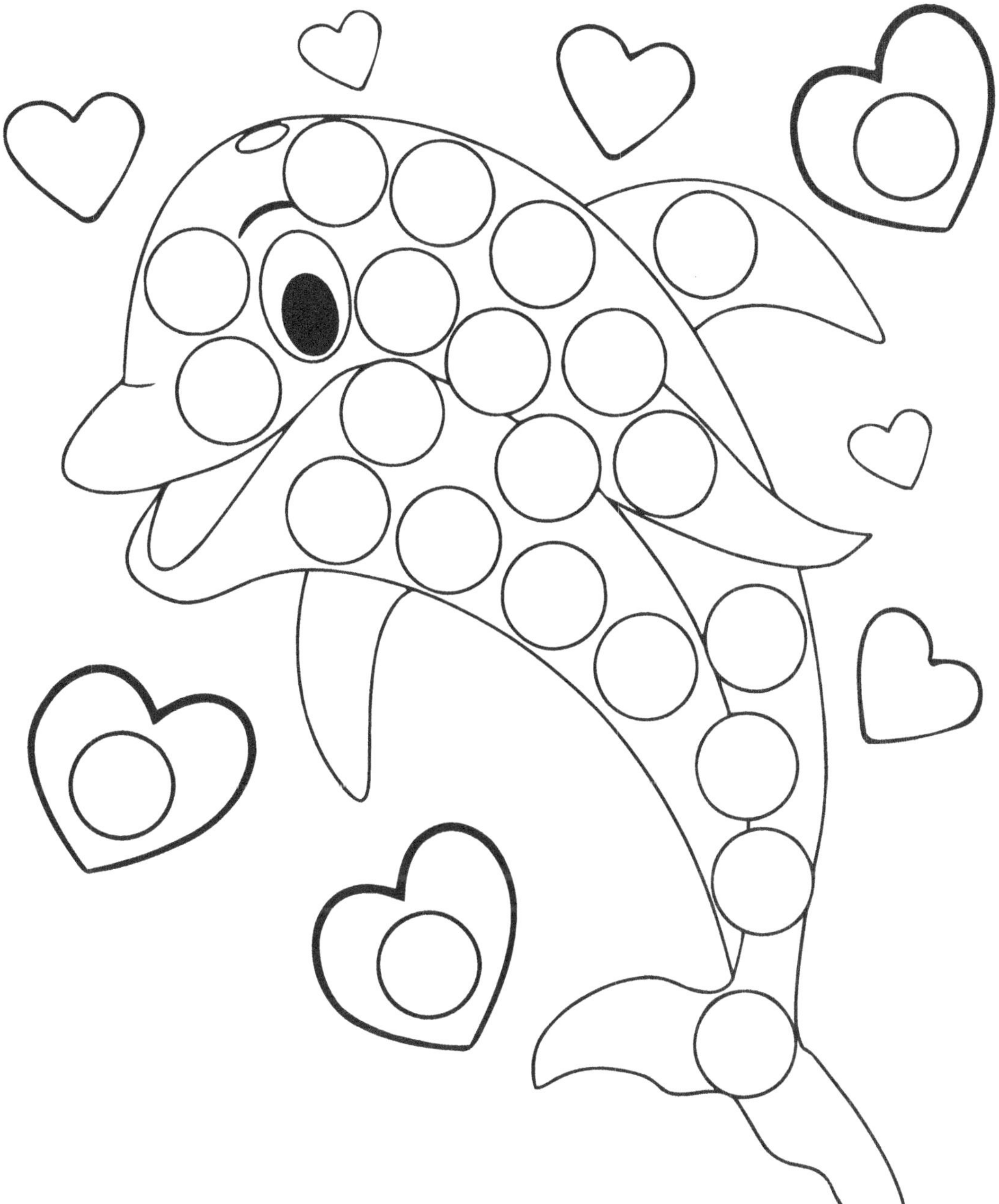

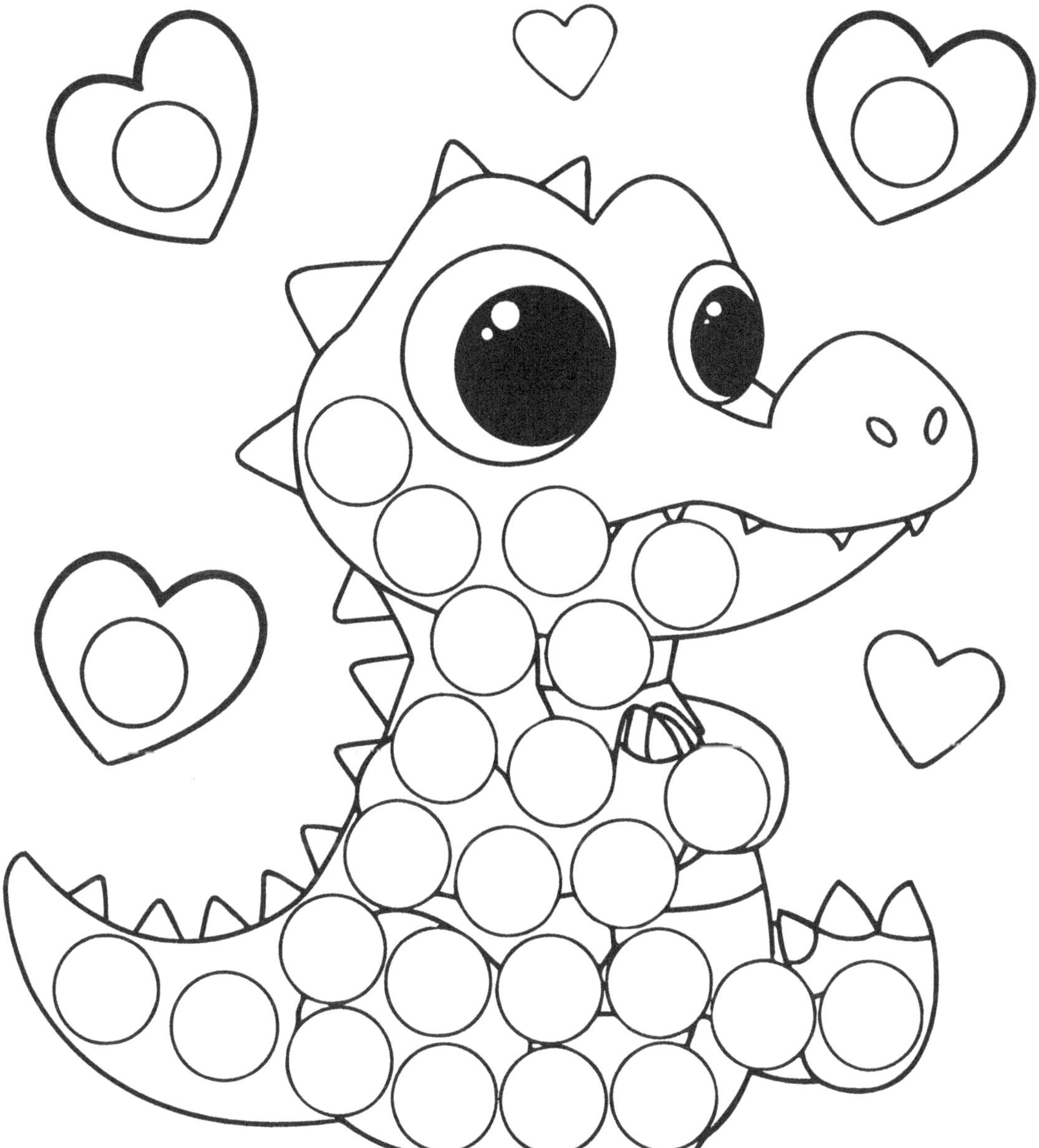

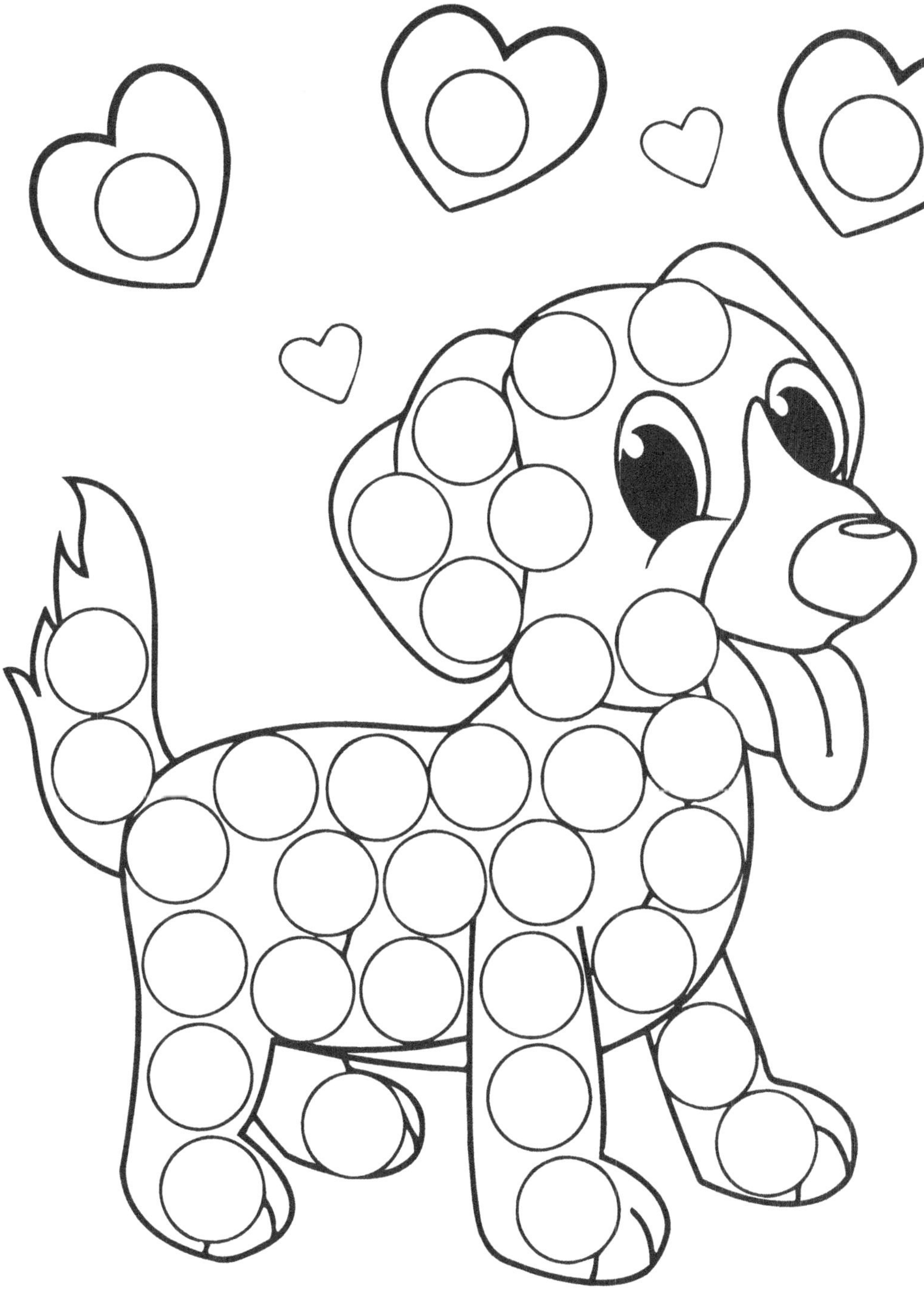

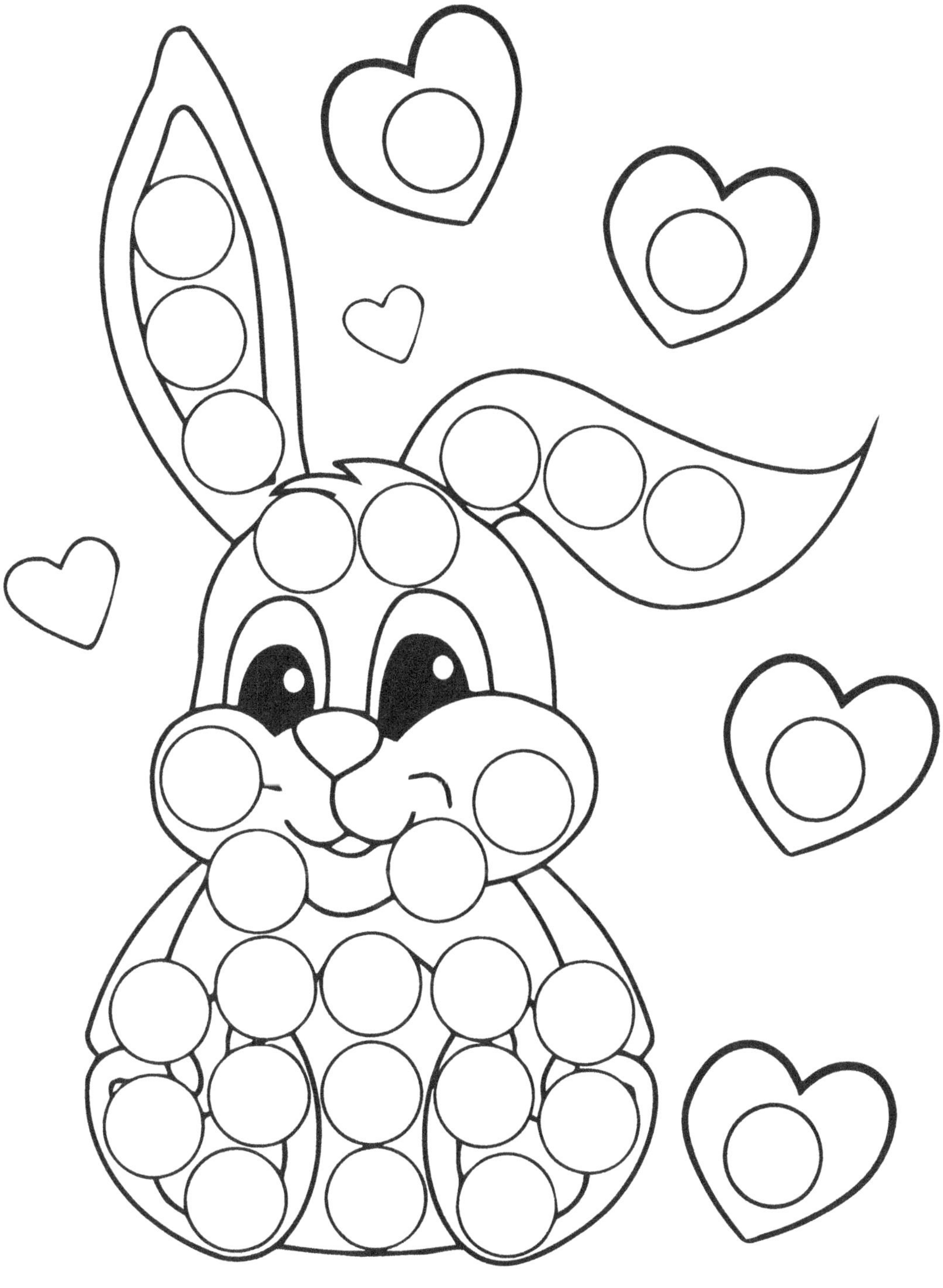

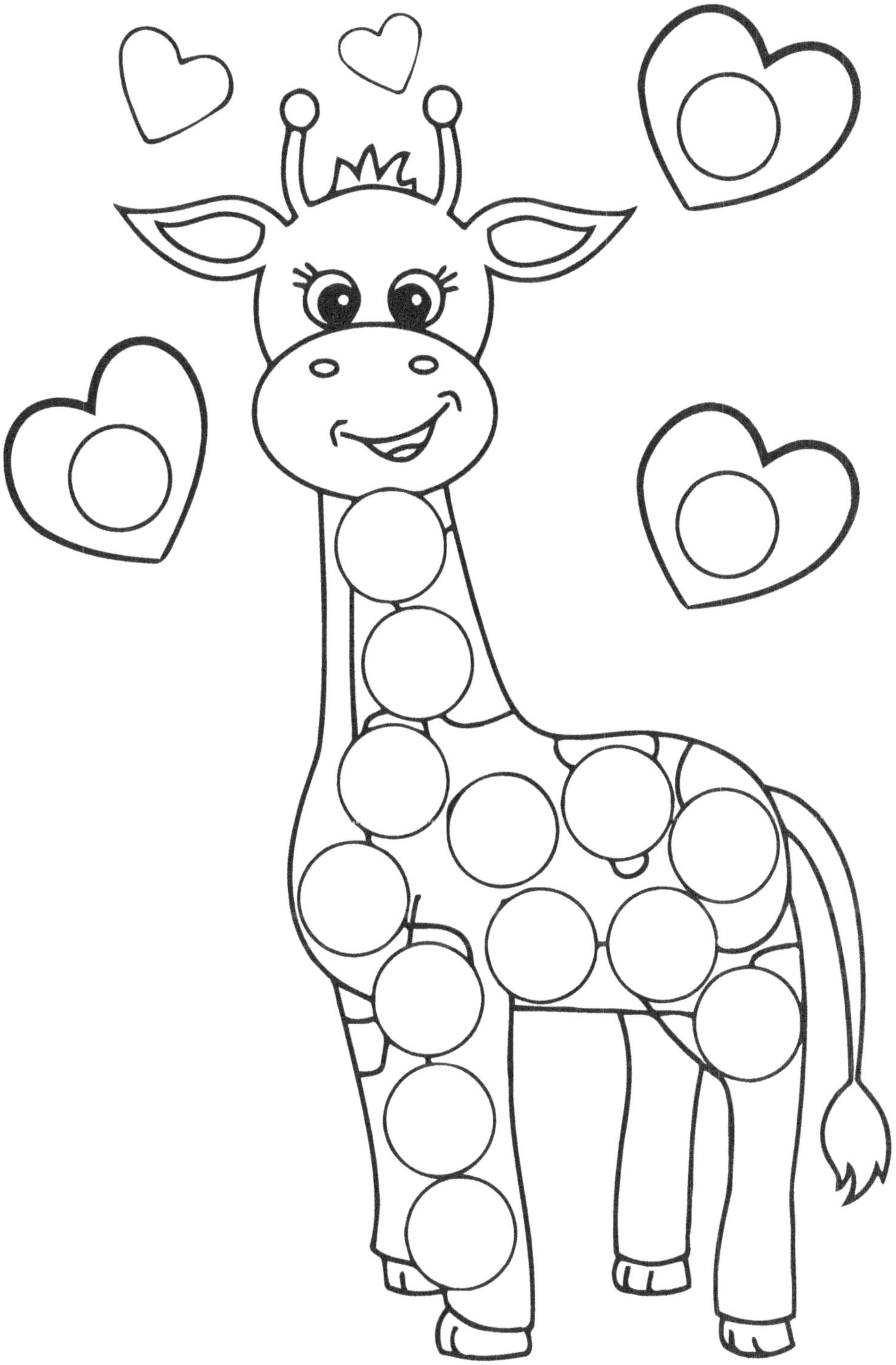

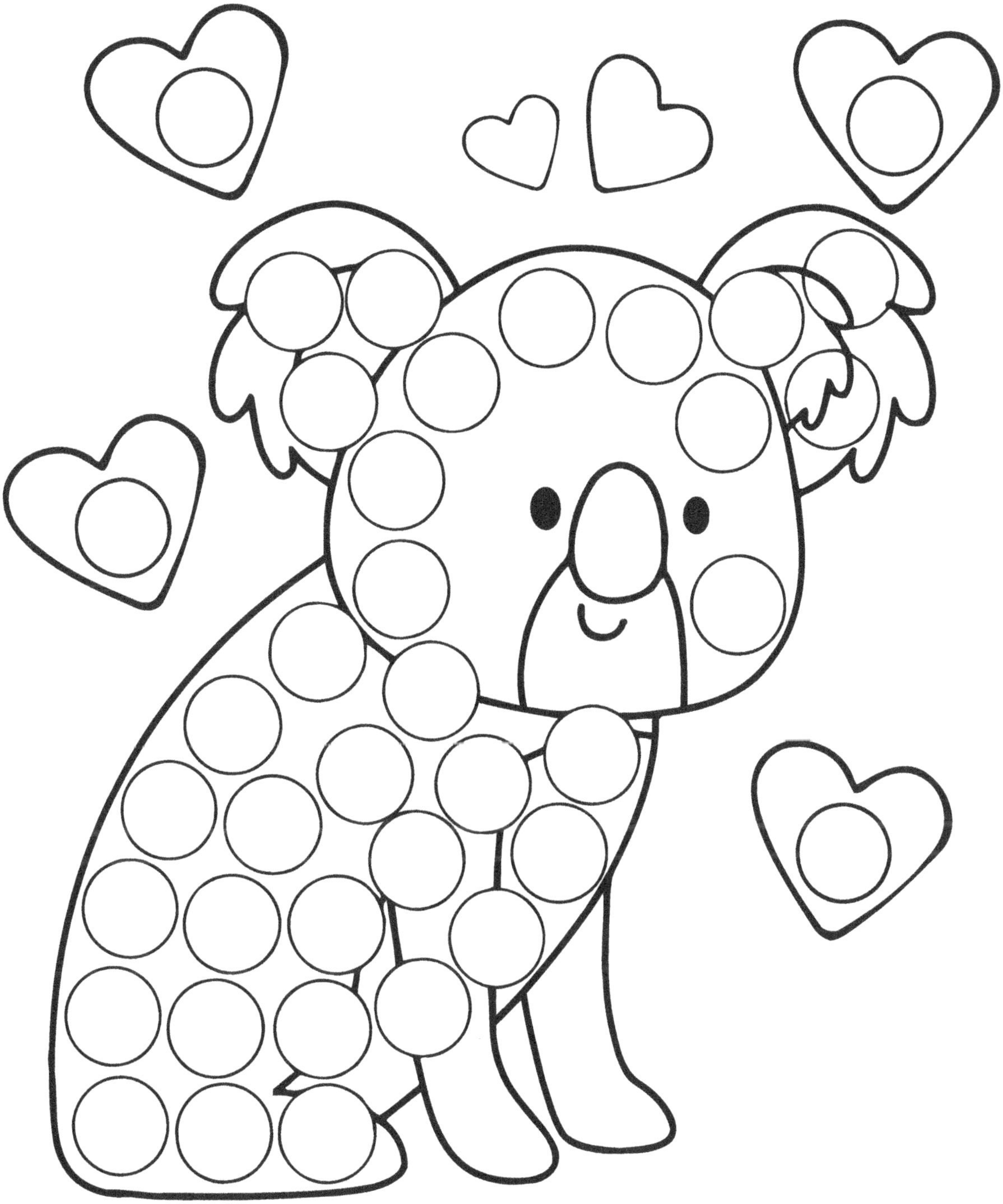

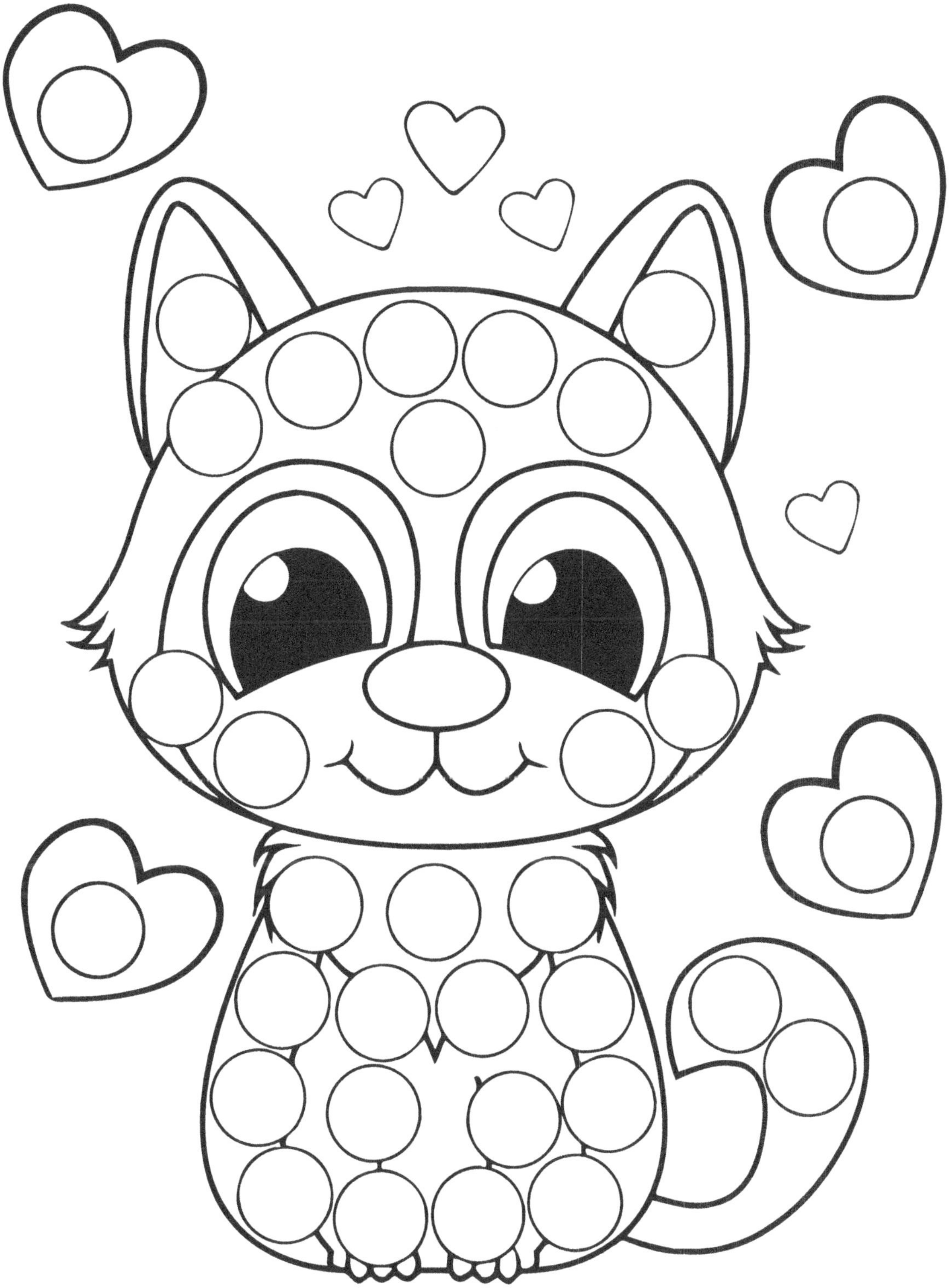